The Complete Guide to Options & Day Trading

This Go To Guide Shows The Advanced Strategies And Tactics You Need To Succeed To Day Trade Forex, Options, Futures, and Stocks

By David Hewitt & Andrew Peter

"The Complete Guide to Options & Day Trading: This Go To Guide Shows The Advanced Strategies And Tactics You Need To Succeed To Day Trade Forex, Options, Futures, and Stocks" Written by "David Hewitt & Andrew Peter".

The Complete Guide to Options & Day Trading is a bundle of the books "The Advanced Day Trader Guide" & "Options Trading for Beginners".

Hope You Enjoy!

The Advanced Day Trader Guide

Follow the Ultimate Step by Step Day Trading Strategies for Learning How to Day Trade Forex, Options, Futures, and Stocks like a Pro for a Living!

David Hewitt & Andrew Peter

Table of Contents

Introduction

Congratulations for purchasing The *Advanced Day Trader: Follow the Ultimate Step by Step Day Trading Strategies for Learning How to Day Trade Forex, Options, Futures, and Stocks like a Pro for a Living!* and thank you for doing so.

The following chapter will discuss why day trading. You will know why day trading is essential and how you can conduct it to achieve your primary aim.

There are numerous books on this topic out there in the market, thanks again for choosing this one!

Every effort made it is to make sure that it is as much full information as possible, please enjoy

Why trading;

Trading is the buying as selling of sound as well as service. You need to be active in the participation of the practices that you can do in the financial market. The more successful you are likely to depend on your ability to make a profit in a certain period. The time that you will decide to engage in trade will be valuable on the strategy that you will use and the advantage that you are going to make.

Day trading will give you a chance to open as well as several close positions in a day. While in swing trade, trade is likely to take a few days and can even go for weeks or months. The two trade types can work best for you, but it will depend on your capability. The time that you have will determine the trade that you will involve in since some take more time than the other. The circumstances that you are in will dictate the deal that will suit you. The swing will accumulate gains as well as losses in a slower than day trading.

Chapter 1: How Day Trading Works

Day Trading vs. Swing Trading

Day trading is the purchase, as well as sales of a commodity within one trading day. It is more likely to happen in the stock and foreign exchange market.

Swing trading is the buying and selling of a stock that indicates either an upward or a downward movement in the days to come.

Some differences you will see in between the two forms of trade. The differences include:

Risk

Day trading is riskier and can make the debts to accumulate faster. The day traders use margin that leads to high profit, and when it comes to losses, they go a massive failure. The money that you will use in day trading will be borrowed, and when you go a loss, it will hit you hard. When it is your first time in the trade, you heed to be careful because you are likely to make loses fast. When you get in the market without adequate of how you will run it, you will be practicing gambling.

Swing trading does not rely on borrowed money and so you no need to worry about how you will offset any debt. There are lesser chances for you to lose your money since there are numerous approaches on how to manage the risks.

Time Commitment

Day trading will need you to be fully committed, and it will take a considerable amount of your time. As a trader, it requires you to change your positions in small time intervals. You need to do so to make sure that you are in a place to make a good profit. Such kind of commitment will make you have a lot of stress. You will not have much time for your daily activities since it is a full commitment. You need to be alert always so that you can know when the market is open. The time is limited to trade and only specific hours of the day that the deal can happen.

Swing trading makes use of time frames, which are a bit longer. You can hold your security for a few days or even at times weeks. Despite that you need to monitor your position so that you can make a profit, you will have enough time to adjust. You can do swing trading as a part-time job while as you undertake other responsibilities. That level of flexibility will work better for you if you want to make a profitable trade without involving your too much time. There is no time limit when you do a deal. You can look for trades and place your order at any time, even when the market closes.

Stress

Day trading has an association of weight since you need to make sure that you are in a safe position. You need to have discipline and be decisive when dealing with such markets. You have to put in hard-work since you are competing with professionals who have devoted their life in day trading.

Swing trading, on the other hand, can be even appropriate to people who have little knowledge about finance. There is less stress associated with this, and for someone not ready for full-time trading can practice swing trade. It is a better option and less risky.

Startup Cost

When you get in day trading, you are likely to compete with high-frequency traders as well as market professionals. Such people will do everything within their ability to have trading advantages. If you desire to get into the trade, you will need to put in place a state-of-the-art software. You as well need to have a platform and up-to-date technology. Swing trade does not require such significant startup capital. You need to have either a computer or a laptop. Conventional trading items are all that you require getting into the trade. You do not have to sweat so much when looking for how to find your way.

Buying Long, Selling Short

When there are price changes in any stock despite the direction it takes, there will be either loss of profit. The reason behind this is the variance of buying long and selling short. The aim that everyone has when getting into a trade is to buy when the prices are low and sell when the prices shoot. That will make sure that there is some profit out of any business that we conduct. Nevertheless, some investors do vice versa.

Buying Long

Anytime that you buy a stock, you do that hoping that at the moment you will be selling, it will have risen. When you do a proper survey on stock, you are likely to make a high return. You need to buy a share and hold it for some time as you await its prices to go up. Buying long positions and holding them for a long time will give you a good return.

A long trader always hopes that the price of any asset that they dispose of will have a price increment. They are forever standing in an open position, and they can go long. When they go long, they will be no limitations on their profit potential since the asset price can go up any time. The risk their stock is getting to zero is limited. When they make several small moves, they are likely to make a profit and can control the risks as well as gains.

Buying long is the method that is, in most cases, made use in the market. When you invest in buying long, you will reap good profits within a short period. The profit made need not for anyone to work extra hard. You will dispose of the stock once the price in the market goes to the levels that you desire.

Selling Short

Pessimists, as well as opportunists, like it when they are selling quickly, and that is how they play. When someone wants to sell short, they do that intending to sell high prices and buy back at lower prices. They don't sell their shares, but they sell borrowed shares. Some companies will lend you the shares when you open an account with them. You are not the real person who poses the shares, but for the period you own them, you can lend them. A short seller can borrow them and put them to sale in an open market. The short sellers will be needed to pay interest to the brokerage company that has to lend them the shares. The interest rates will be different o the size of the account. The short seller always hopes that the prices will fall with times so that they can buy and put for sale. That will make them have big profits making it worth them being in the business.

When you get into selling short, you sell an asset before buying it with the hopes that the prices will drop. When you get into short selling, you will have to pay interest on the money that you will borrow. The money you use to do trading is not your own since it is acquired and so the need to pay for dealing with it. The interest will accumulate during the period that you are holding stock. For you to realize a profit when you are in short selling, the proceeds need to be higher than the cost. Your statement will not change when you borrow the shares, and you have not put them on sale. That will mean that you like the short seller, you will have a short position on the stock that you borrowed.

Retail vs. Institutional Traders

The Capacity of an Investor

Retail traders deal with the stock of small size since it has a low price, making it attractive to them. That will make them buy numerous different securities so that they can get a diversified profit. They make use of technical analysis systems that make use of the behavior of the past price, patterns as well as indicators. That will help them to predict the possible movement of the prices in the future. When they are not able to make a considerable amount of profit, they will blame their poor psychology. They do not agree to own the losses they make, and they blamed the market. They will do this as a way to protect their ego. They forget that failures are part of trade, and they can incur it at any given time. Retail traders use revenge, and they will expect big profits from that. A new person in this trade with no necessary training as well as skills, will not necessarily make a profit of a considerable amount.

Institutional traders will not depend on any indicators so that they can know the price movements. They focus on the principals as well as sentiment while paying attention to the ways to manage risk. They as well concentrate on keeping appropriate trading psychology. Such a trader will put their primary focus on managing risk but will rarely make use of revenge. Revenge has a high chance that they can lose the money, and for that, they are extra careful if they use revenge.

Retail traders have no much capital to help them support the basic needs that they have to cater to. That will make them make too much risk since they will make use of leverage. If they use force, they will have to take more precautions because they may lose a lot than when they do not use leverage. They always think that when they leverage the traders, they will get more profit very quickly. When you are new in the market, you will make huge loses, which may discourage you from continuing in the trade. They will develop poor habits that will take quite some time to break.

Retail traders do not know that they need to have consistency professionally. When you develop the right track record, you will be in a better position to gain respect. That is known to be vital than even making vast amounts of profit. You can get into a trade with money that you do not want to lose, and you make a good profit. Such pressure is too high for some traders

Institutional traders will have excellent capital backup and are likely to get more capital. When they show consistency as well as improve their record, they are likely to receive more capital. Such traders will pay money so that they can get the news about the market in a fast way. They will do that so that they will be a mile away from their competitor.

Retail traders will pay no attention to pay news, and they will not have the interest to know how the economic data is going on. The best trading opportunities were when they were e share put in the news. That will make this trader feel shame, and they will not have a chance to know where they will dispose of their stock.

Institutional traders will put their focus on developing as well as maintaining excellent trading psychology. That makes them look forward and have a focus on things that are of importance to them when it comes to trading in real-time. Institutions will go to the extent of paying psychologists so that they can keep the traders mentally active as well as have a focus.

High-Frequency Trading (HFT)

It is a trading platform that makes use of powerful computers to make large transactions at an extremely high speed. Complex algorithms are put to use to help analyze several markets as well as execute the orders based on the market condition. The traders that can achieve things first are likely to earn more profit than the ones that perform at a slow speed. The trading system will send the stock out there when they know the direction in which the market is heading.

High-frequency will be familiar when there is the introduction of incentives from exchanges. It aims at adding liquidity in the market, and the cash increases when there is an addition of more incentives. That will mean that the profit levels will go up beside their favorable spreads. Multiplying the complimentary range by a significant number of traders in each day will translate to a considerable profit for the high-frequency traders.

Some will view this as an unethical as well as an unfair advantage that the large firms have against small investors. High-frequency trading disrupts the effect of fairness for the technology that is put to use has abusive strategies. Traders will take advantage of the gap between the supply and demand and use the speed to manipulate the rest of the traders. There is no fundamental base of the company or any prospects that they make to grow. Nevertheless, there are chances that you can strike an opportunity.

HFT has no specific target and can cause collateral damage at any time to retail traders, and there investors who buy and sell in large quantities. It will be accessible when the exchanges offer incentives. With the high number of transactions that are made in a day, that translates to high amounts of profit. Some advantages are in attachment with the high-frequency trading. They include and not limited to;

It trades in significant numbers of securities and gives a trader the chance to make a profit. That will be so even when there are little price fluctuations. The trading algorithms are in charge of scanning several markets as well as exchanges. That will give the trader the chance to get more trading opportunities.

It is known to enhance liquidity because competition increases in the market. That is possible since the trades are conducted in a fast way, and the number of transactions made will relatively go high. When the liquidity goes up, the bid-ask tends to decline, and that makes the market to have an efficient price.

However, some risks come with the high-frequency trading and they include;

It is a controversial activity, and little is agreed among the people involved. Though it is known to create liquidity, it has a critic that the cash is a ghost. It is not real since the securities are not held, not even for a little time. An investor can buy a security that has gone under trading for several times. The high-frequency traders will make a profit at the expense of the small traders. That makes it hard for small traders to thrive as well as grow in the competitive world.

There are links of high-frequency trading with the volatility of a market that can even make it to crash. Some of the traders will engage in illegal practices like spoofing as well as layering. That makes it evident that high-frequency trading will make there to be high volatility that will not help a trader to survive in the market. That will be a way to eliminate new as well as small investors, making it an unfair game.

Trade Best, Leave the Rest

You give it your best and make sure that you will not regret later on. You need to look for the stock that will provide you with the best returns and the one that will not incur a lot of expenses. Every trader gets in the market so that they can make a profit and find a way of living. No one wants to get into the trade, and they get losses. It is the wish of every investor to invest in a market that will have returns. Get the best stock that you know will not be an obstacle in your moving forward. Put it out there, whether in the open or closed market and make sure that you have an attractive strategy to make it attract potential buyers.

Take your time to explore the exact ting that people need out here so that you can fill in the gap. You should not let the demand in the market to surpass the supply. That will mean that you are not active in one way or the other. Trading the best is all that you need to focus on so that you will make the best out of the chance that you have.

The trade that will favor you depending on the time and your availability is what you need to involve in. Your capacity is what will make you get into the market out there, and you start trading. However, you do not need to go to trade without an aim. Your focus is what will determine whether you will be successful or not. Your zeal to find out more and research more about the market is what will make you thrive in the trade.

The stock or securities that you suppose will not give you profit should be the last thing that you need to think about. Some investments will make you have losses all the time, regardless of the effort you inject in them. That will demoralize you, and you feel there is no need to be in the trade anymore. That is the kind of business that you need to disconnect from so that you can save your energy and time.

Some are the cases when you get in trade, and you realize that you are not making any profit and losses at all. That will cause you to stagnate, meaning that you will see no benefit of investing in such a stock. You can opt to get into a trade where you will need to borrow money so that you can involve in business. You need to when it comes to such a case because you can end you incurring huge losses if you will not be prudent.

There are cases when you need to chip in the extra effort so that out can make the best out of the trade. You can pay a psychologist so that you will keep the business mentally active. If that is the only way to get the best in business, you do not need to hesitate to do that. If you suffer financial losses and you never graduate to another status, and you begin to make a profit, you need to leave that trade. That will never be seen as a good trade. Bear in mind that you should trade best and leave alone the rest. The rest involves all the things that are subjecting you to losses regularly. The things that are making you not achieve what you aim for, you need to consider leaving them as well. When you are working independently, you will have an excellent chance to trade best and leave the rest.

Chapter 2: Risk and Account Management

Risk Management Techniques for Day Trading

Risk management is critical in the sense that it helps in cutting down loses. In most cases, it helps a trader to account for all the drops that might be incurred in the trading process. The risks that traders engage in becomes real when a loss is suffered. However, if the risks are managed effectively, the trader gets more profits, and the threats turn out to be an investment. Thus, as a trader, it is always wise to be vigilant and make effective plans. It is wise to avoid making decisions or taking risks that might ruin your business altogether. However, as a trader, having strategies as well as objectives that offer the guidelines towards success. It is good to incorporate risk management strategies in your practice to avoid cases where one suffers excessive loses. It is worth noting that trade can be exciting, especially when you are making profits. However, the best practice is to stay focus with due diligence, and with the time, you will be able to cope up with situations such as loses.

Take a look at some of the techniques that traders can use to manage risks.

Planning your Trades

There is a Chinese saying that claims that a battle is won before it is fought. In other words, the best military forces plan on how to win before they engage in the real fight. In the same way, successful traders always expect their trade. Just like in a row, panning ahead brings all the difference between those who fail and those who succeed.

In most cases, planning helps one to identify the potential risks that might be ahead. Also, one can foresee the dangers that lie ahead and gets prepared. As you engage in trade, make sure that your broker is right for frequent trading. It is worth noting that successful traders know what to sell and the price they will be selling the goods with. In other words, they plan for success right away after receiving the raw-materials.

In most cases, a trader who fails in business doesn't have a clear outline of what they need in the trade. Any mission or any drive doesn't lead them. Most of them don't have a target of rather a profit margin that dictates their plans.

In most cases, they are in business with the wrong mindset hence the continuous loses. Unsuccessful traders engage in risks without any intention.

In most cases, they engage in the transaction without taking consideration of the markets therein. They are some who engage in business activities that are less profiting with an aim that things will over-turn. In other words, they don't create some time to study their markets before starting. Thus, as a trader, make a point of doing some marketing researches before taking any risk. Such a study is critical in the sense that it helps in effective planning.

Consider the One Percent Rule

It is worth noting that most traders who have succeeded in various marketing economies use the rule of one percent to be effective. The government suggests that one should never use more than 1% of the capital in a single trade. In other words, if you have $10,000 in your trading account, your utilization or rather the instruments of use shouldn't more than $100. Although the rule is commonly used by individuals who have more than $100,000in their raiding account, it is good to consider such plans to avoid any cases where funds are over-used.

Setting Stop-Loss and Take – Profits Points

It is good to adopt a culture where one aims at making fewer profits and incurring low loses. A set stop loss point refers to a situation where a trader sells goods at a lower price than the intended one. The aspect occurs when the plans fail to work out. However, one ought to learn from the mistake and come up with ways that will prevent such situations from occurring. On the other hand, a take-profit point refers to a situation where a trader sets at a price and ends up making the profit of the trade. The trader is forced to come up with measures that ensure that such benefits are made from the premises.

Diversify the Hedge

There is trading saying that advice traders not to put all the eggs in one basket. The aspect is linked to the fact that there are times when things backfire and a significant loss sets in. Thus, you may end up collapsing in the long last. Therefore, the art of risking requires one to diversify and ensure that the risks are equally distributed. More investment should be made to the activity, or rather, the step is taken. Dangers should be taken in markets that are relevant available.

Compare Investment Accounts

It is not good to engage in different trades without comparing or instead of checking how they have been progressing in recent years. In other words, it is good to consider the profits as well as the loses being incurred on the premises. The aspect is critical in the sense that it allows one to prepare for the incoming loses. It is good to consider several options before making the decision on which trade favors you. It is worth noting that when you are a beginner in an individual market, there are chances that you will be overwhelmed and expected to make instant profits. However, it is worth noting that such situations don't exist and you may engage in business and make loses for the first few months, however, the art of comparing different investment accounts is critical in the sense that it allows the trader to make the decisions that are sound and effective. In other words, the aspect ensures that the trader engages in the best business there is.

In a nutshell, you shouldn't engage in any business for the sake of doing it. However, have plans and compare different options before making a decision that is more of profit-making.

Account Management Techniques for Day Trading

The art of managing an account is trading is never secure. In other words, the art of trading within a single day may attract several issues that need to be addressed adequately. Day trading, in most cases, is challenging, considering that there are days when one makes profits or loses. There are cases where plans backfire, and massive losses are incurred. However, the best thing to do is to plan for the future and make the necessary adjustment that is critical in trading. It is worth noting that day trading becomes profitable when traders take it seriously and conduct researches. Take a look at some of the techniques that are critical in managing the accounts of a day to day business.

Knowledge is Power

Even if you are making day to day profits, you need to keep learning. In other words, also, if you are familiar with all that is required, it is good to keep adding more skills to your premises. The aspect is linked to the fact that the more one gest updated, the better. It is good to keep walking around and benchmarking in different areas. The element is critical in the sense that one can comprehend what other people keep doing to increase inner profit-making. It is wise to keep

21

masking and making more of clarifications rather than pretending to be knowing everything and end up failing.

Set Aside Funds

In as much as you are earning from different places, it is good to be wise and save some coins. In other words, after making huge profits, it is god not to consume all but consider the changes that are expected. Saving is critical in the sense that it may compensate for the places where loses are incurred.

Set Aside Time

Day trading requires more of your time. In other words, you need to be vigilant and make the necessary decisions or, rather, arrangements that will ensure that you are around your day trading. Some aspects can`t be achieved unless one is present. Thus, one ought to be vigilant enough and ensure that you are making the necessary adjustments while working. Although one might be caught up with issues and fail to be available. However, one ought to make plans required to ensure that arrangements are made active and your presence is prioritized. The aspect is critical in the sense that it allows the close monitoring of the business; hence few loses that are as a result of errors.

Start Small

It is worth noting that Rome wasn't built in one day. In other words, even if you need to have a big business, you need to start smack and allow the process of growth to take place. It is worth noting that without patience, the company might collapse. Thus, as you start your plans, ensure that you start small and keep investing as time goes by. The aspect allows one to identify the gap there is and make a pint of staying it effectively.

Avoid Penny Stocks

In most cases, when engaging in day trading, you will aim at making profits and spending less. However, that is not a guarantee that you should stock penny stock so as you may make profits. It is good to choose quality and make sound choices. In other words, make a point of stocking goods of high quality and expect to make supernormal profits.

Timing

It is worth noting that no trade remains in the peak season for the entire year. In other words, there is a day when the season is relatively low. However, if you are experienced, you will learn that there are times when one makes supernormal profits. Ensure that at this time, you have all that is required. It is good to recognize the pattern in the market and work with them.

Cut losses with Limit Orders

It is good to decide on what kind of law you will be taking. In other words, it is wise to ensure that all the riders made are well investigated to check on the expenses incurred and the profits expected. In other words, one ought to consider the benefits of each order. Thus, to avoid more loses, one should take a trade or rather an order that is fulfilling the expectations of both the seller and the buyer. Such aspects are critical in the sense that it allows one to avoid making huge loses when supplying or meeting the needs of the orders that might not be paid or may be delayed in terms of compensation. However, one may concentrate on more promising meeting order, and that is sure. The aspect is critical in the sense that it opens the minds of an individual and exposes one to the things that are critical in business.

Be Realistic

It is worth noting that a strategy doesn't have to win at all times to be effective. In other words, you don't have to keep changing your plans if an approach fails to bring in some aspects of profits. It is worth noting that a project may win today and incur a loss in another day. However, that is not a guarantee that this will, be the trend forever. Therefore, it is good to be patient and be real by comprehending that days are different and losses and profits are real. Therefore as you are engaging in this day to day business, entire that you are fresh and operate in the right way. Stick to your plan and have something that is driving you. It is worth noting that successful traders move very fast and don't overthink much. In other words, you don`t have to change the strategy so as you may keep winning. However, you need to be vigilant and make some basic plans that will favor you. It is wise to follow your formula wisely rather than copying what other people are doing. Work with your line and specialize and turn out to be unique and attract more clients.

Trading Psychology

Trading is the most significant endeavor that one can engage in. The aspect is due to the fact that one meets a lot of issues that challenge one`s life. Other customers are life-threatening while as some smile at a person. All these aspects are commonly found in trade. In other words, it is a profession that sharpens the minds of an individual and opens up someone as well. The psychological aspect of trading is essential. In other words, the art of thinking faster and making the right decisions within a short period is critical in several issues. It is good to invest one`s time in undertaking a gig that motivates them in business and avoids the gear of fear that may affect the way one interacts with traders as well as customers. In other words, the art of being courageous and facing trade with the utmost faith that all will be well is essential.

Take a look at some of the aspect that is important in understanding the art of trade psychology

Understating Fear

When traders receive bad news about anything, shock and confusion sets in. One is left wondering what to do next. In most cases, one is forced to leave whatever they are doing to do and cater to the news that approaches from the premises. However, as a good trader, you need to understand what fear is and respond appropriately. In other words, it is worth noting that fear is a natural reaction that is perceived when something happened in life. It is worth noting that one can't avoid as well as calamities in trade. There are days where accidents occur, and one might lose everything. There are other cases where good go wrong, and one is forced to incur a loss. It is worth noting that the art of quantifying fear is essential. In other words, the art of understanding the factor that is causing concern and the reason behind this fear is necessary. It is good to ponder the issue that is causing anxiety as fast as possible. In other words, if you fear that there is something terrible that might be appearing in your trade, you need to be prepared and make the necessary changes that might help curb the issue. The aspect may include avoiding a particular route of business or failing to supply or make the same orders. Despite all the sensations, the best thing to do as a trader is to ensure that everything is fresh, and one maintains the focus that acts as a driving force.

Overcoming Greed

There is an adage that claims that even pigs get slaughtered. In other words, pigs are known to be some of the greediest animals. However, it reaches a point where the pigs are killed and eaten by other human beings despite their greedy nature. In the same way, if you are grasping in trade, there are chances that one-day things might backfire and you may end up losing all the investments made in the entire year or period of occupation. In trade, greed can be devastating as the trader runs the risk of getting whipped by a single blow. In other words, if one isn't careful, the greedy aspect of trade may run a trader into a ditch that one may never recover from. Thus, before making any decision, make a point of doing some sought of investigation and learn how to be patient with whatever you have been doing. The aspect is linked to the fact that there are traders who engage in business simply because they had that there are a lot of profits. In most cases, they will participate in the market without knowing what is required on the premises.

Setting Rules

Unless there are rules that are governing what you are doing, there are chances that you might fall. In other words, even if you are your boss, you need to understand that there are other traders you are competing with. The aspect indicates that you need to have some guidelines that will govern the activities you are doing. The element is critical in the sense that it helps one avoid cases where funds are used in inappropriate manners. You don't have to be emotional when things fail to work. However, with the necessary guidelines, you will be an excellent position to evade the loss as policies are guiding you in the same. The arty of doing things without a plan or rather guidelines leads one into the art of making loses at all times. It is worth noting that planning includes the funds to use as well as the time to dedicate to the trade. It is worth noting that working for long hours isn't a guarantee that you will succeed. However, the art of working smart plays a critical role in ensuring that a trader achieves all that is required in life. Even if you have a family, it is wise to set the limits over the funds they will be using. In other words, you don't have to use the entire profits simply because you are your boss. However, it is even wise to have an accountability partner that will guide you in the things to do. Be open to such people and allow them to advise you accordingly. It is wise to be deliberate and make the right decisions. However, all this depends on the emotion as well as the perception you have. It is also wise to set targets that will guide you. In case you hit your destination, you don't have to stick with the same limit. However, make a point of concentrating and increase the art of focus. The aspect is linked to the fact that trade requires one to be vigilant and open to new ideas. In other words, keep learning and seeking advice from those who are your seniors. The aspect allows you to work within limits and avoids a lot of loses.

Chapter 3: How to Find Stocks for Traders

Stocks in Play

Remember that trading is very competitive and requires extensive analysis. The stocks of the market have that nature of increasing and decreasing systematically. That is upon you as the buyer to accurately evaluate how the share performs in the trading. In trading, there is an indicator that one must read clearly. The stocks in play here mean they move very fast and needs one who is an accurate speculator

The stock in play may produce excellent revenues and terrible risks, respectively. However, if you are an investor, this is not the best juncture for you, as these stocks are very volatile. Thus it is suitable for the day readers who want quick profits. Remember that there are the stockbrokers who demand the brokerage fee. Therefore, the day traders have to watch on the behavior of the stocks to ensure they amerce a more significant deal of profit.

Characteristics of the Stocks in Play

The stocks in play are volatile. That is one of the main reasons day traders like the stocks in play. Volatility in these shares means that they fluctuate in value more than other portfolios. Therefore, you can trade them and amerce a more significant risk or profit due to their fluctuation. If their indicators clocks on the right pattern, then you will acquire more substantial returns.

That is different from the companies that are meant for investments. These companies show a less deal of a change in the price swings of the shares. That means that they are less volatile. Maybe the period they experience such price swings can be even once per year. Therefore, this requires the traders who are very patients enough in trying to attain the returns. Moreover, you are also secured with less risk because of that low volatility. In a simple sense, if you are an investor who likes striding in slow but sure markets, then this is the best avenue to be.

Another characteristic is that they show a great deal of volume. Just like the volatile amount rises in the stock in play, no wonder higher returns are sometimes experienced. Remember that volume is an essential indicator of the technical analysis that measures the trading price differences and momentum. The higher the size, the more chances of reaching to returns. In another concept, this volume is the number of shares traded over a specified period. Therefore the traders should choose the most liquid stocks. That means that they are mostly convertible to cash. Moreover, for day traders who seek a fast entry and exit from the business, they, therefore, require liquid securities. That is to tell you that if a stock does not have a liquidity level, then the broker is incapable of negotiating a good deal with the buyer.

How to Use Stock in play

Most of the stocks become in play as a result of a situation like a news announcement where they become massively traded. However, do not judge the trading basing on that news because you can predict the price moment. Naturally, you would expect that the share prices will fall as a result of the adverse outcomes. Contrary to that, these shares may rise to the surprise of the shares undesirable news hence making them unpredictable. Always check to know the price movement of the stock in play. Therefore, you have to recognize the best type of indicator applicable.

To have a proper stock in play, first, know the technical terms used. These terms may include the bear market, breakdown, or breakout; that is where the stock breaks below the previous lows or heights, respectively. Others are the dividends, breakeven points, and many other terms.

You should also know the type of indicator used, which includes the RSI, MACD, and Stoichiometric oscillator and many others. After knowing all these technicalities, check the price movement using a demo trial and try to trade. Make it as a trial and error until you assess the change of pattern and the trend of the shares. Know the particular juncture you will score big in the market. Finally, make a trade after realizing that.

Float and Market Cap

You may have seen an advertisement for a stock exchange market either in the newspaper. Do you take time to think about the capacity of the shares that a company has given to be traded? Moreover, do you know that other stocks are not supposed to be sold? In that case, the market capitalization is the total value of the outstanding company's share that can be traded. The outstanding shares are the shares owned by the shareholders or other stakeholders. They usually are priced by the market price index of a company.

The floating market cap is the shares that take into account the type of stocks that are released for the public subscription. That means the shares you see advertised in the newspapers are sometimes the free float shares. That should exclude the restricted shares which must not be traded. These assets include the stocks owned by the insiders, promoters, or government. The free-float market cap is a technique for measuring the market capitalization.

Factors Affecting the Market Cap and How to Calculate It

To calculate the market cap of the day, one should multiply the outstanding shares with the market index of the day. Therefore, the factors which affect the market cap should affect either of these two domains, which are the outstanding shares and the market price.

In that case, factors that affect the number of these outstanding shares include, first, the issue of the new shares, which are entirely different from the initial shares. When new shares are traded sometime, they have a higher value. Or they can win a more considerable profit margin as customer's trade are enticed to feel a taste of their trading.

Another determiner is the buyback share where the firm wishes to purchase the shares it had sold to subscribers or its shareholders. That is a move to replace paying of dividends to those shareholders as they view bonus is an expensive way of returning cash to the shareholders.

Concerning the market price index, it is affected by the following factors. One factor is the demand and supply of the shares. That is to mean, if there is a higher demand for the stocks, than the price will be low and vice versa. The strength of the company in terms of its revenue determines the price index too. You can also compare the competitor performance with that of the company to fix the price of the share in achieving that competitive edge. Lastly, there are macro factors that are above the firms' abilities. That includes the government laws on the trading assets or politics of the land.

How to Calculate the Free-Floating Shares

These shares are obtained as the subtraction of the outstanding shares with the restarted shares. Then you can multiply your results with the market index of the company. You can even obtain the percentage of the stocks by dividing the free float shares with the outstanding shares. The results of that can be multiplied with a hindered to know that percentage.

Some of the most notable factors of the free float shares are the management decisions and government influence. For example, the government or the management may redeem that restricted stocks as unrestricted, thereby increasing that float. Moreover, a firm can influence its assets by selling more of them in the secondary offering.

Premarket Gappers

Hey, do not be in that big rush to complete a trade. First, check on the behavior of the market before placing the odds or your account. By having the premarket, you will know the trend and the price or volume movement of the market. That is where you will realize the profitable area to place your fortunes.

Just as you identify the niches or opportunities in the market, thus the same applies to stock trading. These gaps must be determined before making a trade. They are usually the specific place in the chart where the stocks move sharply up or down with a little trading sense. Therefore the assets show the intensity of the gap that can analyze when trading in that stock. Intelligent speculators and investors know too well how to utilize the stated differences.

How to Use the Gappers

As it is already said of the relevance of these gappers. One has to utilize this golden chance to harness a sizeable profit accurately. Remember that activity must be den before the trading exercise. If you are a learner, you must first know the different types of gaps. They include the following.

There is also the breakaways gaps which occur at the end of the price pattern. They also beckon where you should commence new trading. That is relevant, especially to the day traders who like to exit and enter the market with a profit. If the gap were not available, then most traders would be leaving the market with a hefty loss.

Various indicators signal you that it is your last trading attempt. These indicators are the exhaustion gaps. In simple, they are the pointers that identify the end of a price pattern and hints the previous effort.

Some like the common gaps show the area where the price has already gapped. Therefore these indicators do not represent any price trend. Hey, it is not a must for the indicators to identify a danger at the end of closing trading, but the exit point can be discovered in the middle of the trading. Imagine how crucial it would be to discover a threat in the middle of the trade. Therefore you will have ample time to escape the business and prepare yourself adequately. Then that pointer is the continuation gap.

The other step to contemplate is whether to fill or not to fill the gap. Remember, by filling the gap. That means that the price is in the initial gap level. Therefore the technical resistance influences these fills. That is where the price moves up and down sharply.

Another situation is where the initial trading maybe overly constituted that invites for correction. Therefore, this phenomenon is known as irrational exuberance.

The last phenomena are the price pattern. That entails the price movement of the trading. It depends on how it moves or its direction. Features like the continuation and breakaway gaps describe this directional movement. That means these voids are less likely to be filled due to their directional showing character. However, those likes' exhaustion gaps will be filled because they beckon on the price trend endpoint. Therefore, it is upon you the investor to read carefully on the behavior of the trade pattern. Note the exhaustion gap, notably to exit the business and ensure you have attained a profit.

The last stage is the most crucial part where it explains how to play the voids or gap.

Before making that trading, several precautions should be in your mind. These precautions enable you to verify your trading and ensure that there will be no loss in the event. For example, you should realize that once the assets are placed on the selling, it will hardly stop as there is no that immediate support or resistance.

Always identify the directional gaps like the exhaustion and continuation gaps that move in a different course. By the gaps moving in the opposite direction, it makes them tricky to define them. Therefore, remember to classify every kind of gap appropriately.

Follow keenly on the price moving trend and understand the pointers of higher profit points. Know the area you have to exit or enter the market by using the relevant types of those gaps. Analyze the volume trend too accordingly to indicate the gaps present. Always s recognize that the higher volume is associated with the breakaway gaps and the lower amount associated with exhaustion gaps.

Once you have learned that you are ready to start the business, some players will trade on the positivity of the report that will be released concerning the gap up on the next trading day. That is when the crucial factors and key speculators declare good trends of the patterns on the next day. They also identify where to buy the assets either when they are of higher liquid or illiquid. Most of them like to buy liquid stocks ion levels like exhaustion gaps where their shares are easily converted to money upon their exits.

Another way that speculators do is that they will fade the stock in the opposite direction once they establish that the high or low point indicators of the capital have been reached. One strategy they will use is the shorting technique. That involves that when speculators predict a decline in shares, they will borrow them and sell them to other traders. Consequently, the trader will trade on odds that the stocks will decline and can buy them cheaply. Remember that borrowing should be done before the borrowed shares are expected to be returned to the giver.

Real-Time Intraday Scan

Remer that the trading is very diverse, and it needs that control tower or a cockpit that will scan the trade. The term intraday means the act of buying and selling of the stock with n the day. That means the trading day opens and closes the same day or the other day provide the twenty-four hours are not exceeded. The scanners are the programmed computer objects that process the data as instructed. They have the software that processes the values of all the shares you are trading and the transactions involved.

Moreover, they stream the real-time results as the trade continues to take place. To identify the best screener is hard, which needs the help of a professional. However, it is convenient for you to consider the following factors in acquiring the objects.

How to Choose a Stock Scanner

Consider the built-in scanners for the traders who are uncomfortable using their scans. These built-in screeners are programmed according to the trading and the portfolios involved. They have a mastered algorithm and criteria that help in executing a command when needed. If you are that professional trader and you want to save your trading time, consider using this object.

This screener involves the stocks hitting and pointing the new high tradeoff and low tradeoffs, breakeven analysis, and shares crossing moving averages.

Some are the custom scan. The word custom in this context means the personalized content found in those machines. That means you are involved in the making or the programming of the gadget. Therefore you specify the necessary features and characteristics that must be present in that object. If you are using something you had prescribed, then you will feel safe in using change.

These scanners also offer flexibility. That is where the information can be manipulated according to your changing desires of what you want the item to look like.

Consider the filters found in that scanning software. Remember that the professionals use these objects; therefore, they must have updated filtering elements. Filtering in this sense means the classification or analysis of price, volume, EPS, revenue, the behavioral pattern of indicator, and other metrics. The filters are typically found in the scanners. They should also correspond to what the buyer expects; therefore, if your screener is featured with those elements. They also make your work simpler in trading for the shares.

Contemplate how the gadgets can be integrated with other essential information that regards the shares trading. Remember that the objects are used by the end-users who may not be able to analyze the fairing of a share in a market with the constituents. These constituents may include the factors affecting the performance of the stocks, like the news on the price of shares. Some other aspects consist of the type of charts like the candlestick or the variety of indicators available. Therefore, that scanner must have that trading platform that coincides with the correct news and information that affects the behavior of the scales.

Planning the Trade Based on the Scanners

These objects are crucial when trading in the shares. They also simplify your way of analyzing the price, volume, and the indicator in itself. The purpose has that software which may even guide you in making a fruitful trade which will harness good results. That means that it can increase your odds of being successful. Therefore you have to plan accordingly on how to use it the program. The following are ways to initializing their use.

First, you have to adapt to their usage. If you are dealing with a company, teach your subordinate's son how to use it, or you can go for training sections. At other times you should invite experts to help you in buying the right scanners as explained above. The use of customized scanners is better because your desires and preferences will be articulated in the software. Therefore, launch the program and entail its significance to those of your colleagues.

Then plan to install intraday alerts in your device. That should be a mechanism to alarm you about the status of the moving stock or something unique happening in the markets. It is inconvenient as other traders use to check on the market each time of the night to know the trend. How do you think would happen if you sleep at the expense of a great chance to strike the trade. Probably you will feel stressed when you lose a great deal. Therefore, if you have this improvise, they will alert you on a potential winning margin.

Moreover, plan to build watchlists that are concerned with keeping tabs on the behavior of those stocks. Forecast on portfolios that will make you anticipate will perform well in the future. Keeps track of it and crosscheck its response. You can classify a handful of stocks that you like buying. Moreover, it saves time when you want to trade again another day.

Chapter 4: Tools and Platforms

What Broker to Use?

When you want to trade, it is important to make sure that you have a good broker. First, you need to know the type of service you want the broker to offer you and the type of trader you want to be. There are traders who require the broker to manage for them the account and also provide other services such as advice on investment options and research services. If you need such services, it is better to have a full-service broker. This type of broker is good for traders who are new and need much assistance; however, if you trust yourself, you can go for the discounted broker. You should also remember that the risk of investing in trading should be well calculated because you need to have more knowledge of trading and understand the mechanics and trick of trading stock.

In addition, do not just consider the price offered by the broker. Look at how effective the broker will carry out the services that you agree on. It might not be easy at first, but you can seek the advice of a more experienced trader; it can be that he or she knows the connection of good stock brokers. You can get a stockbroker who is cheap in price, but the services offered are inefficient; for example, the execution of a simple trade takes time, and by the time it is executed, the losses have been incurred. Therefore, it is better to have a broker who charges a little bit higher for his services and offers services as promised than to have a cheap broker who does not execute any order in time. These days, it is easier to get brokers online through search. Compare the prices of brokers and the services they are offering, and then choose a broker that offers a good mix of services at a reasonable price, and is reliable and efficient.

Trading Platforms

Trading platforms in stock trading include the traditional platform and online trading platforms. The traditional platforms include the brokers who search for the traders through advertisements in the mainstream media or visiting people in their workplaces and home to persuade them to take up stocks of a particular company. The trading in this platform is most of the time initiated by the broker, who contains all the information concerning which is the best stock to trade in, and the trends and patterns that can be used to make decisions on a particular trade move. The trading in this platform is slow, and the reaction rate to any trade move takes hours because the trader has to inform the broker on the expected move, and the broker executes on behalf of the trade.

The other platforms are online platforms, where everything is done online using a computer or a mobile phone. This platform offers a flexible environment for trading where the trader can do everything for himself or herself or use a broker who manages only the account or the entire trade decisions, depending on the agreement between the trader and the broker. The reaction rate of these platforms is very first with other people devising ways on how to minimize the procedures involved in the execution of important action. In this platform, time is crucial, as delay makes you lose a lot while timely reaction increases your earnings. The traders also have access to a wide range of information that is useful in making crucial decisions of trade and planning for future investment. There are also cases of training done online at a lower cost, where the trader has trained ad when he or she gets enough experience he or she is given a trading account to manage. This platform has made stock trading popular, and individual traders can join the trade with the least amount depending on the brokerage company.

Indicators in Trading

The ABCD Pattern

This is an indicator that makes three swings making line AB and CD that are sometimes referred to as the legs, where BC is the correction line. This pattern presents itself with the BC and CD lines having the same length. The ABCD pattern uses a downtrend, and when it is seen, it shows the trend will be reversed from downward to upward. There are three types of the ABCD trends: the ABCD extension, the classical ABCD pattern, and the AB=CD.

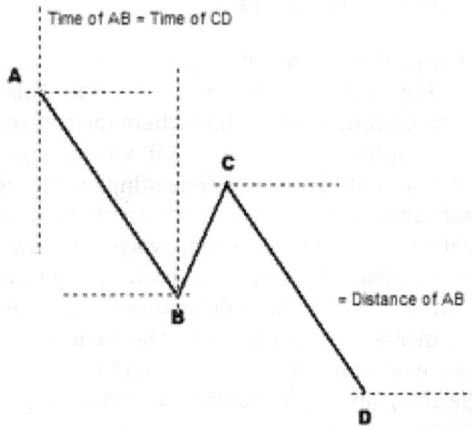

Time of AB = Time of CD

= Distance of AB

AB = CD Pattern

It is important to study the chart until the time when prices reach point D for you enter the trade.

Reversal Trading

This is an indicator that a trend is about to change when the trend in prices of stock wants to change in a trend either from downward to upward from upward to downward. This indicator can be recognized by looking at where the pattern accumulates. If accumulation occurs at the bottom, it shows a reverse in the downward trend, and therefore, buyers start buying to benefit from the anticipated increase in prices of stock. Similarly, if accumulation occurs at the top, the sellers start to sell their stock to avoid losses.

The Moving Average Indicator

This is seen to make use of the moving average in terms of the prices of the stock. An upward inclined moving average indicates an upward trend in the prices of the stock, and when it is seen to incline downwards, it shows the price of the stock is in the upward trend. A downward inclination prompts the seller to sell to reduce losses, while the upward trend shows signals the buyer to buy stock to benefit from the increase in prices of stock. This indicator is easier to use as it allows the buyer or the seller to understand the current shown on the chart and predict whether it will be reversed either downwards or upwards depending on the pattern accumulation.

The Red to Green Indicator

This is an indicator that shows either red or green depending on the difference between the day-break price and its opening price. When the opening price of a stock is lower than the closing price, it gives red lights to show that it is not time to sell the stock; conversely, when the opening price is greater than the closing, it indicates that the sellers can sell because the prices are at the highest. Always use this indicator to trade when you want to trade during the opening hours of opening.

Real-Time Market Data

Stock trading takes place every minute, and therefore volumes of stock are traded every minute, and the prices change from time to time recorded; this record is called real-time market. Real-time market data is the information that is updated on the volume of stock traded, and the updated prices; this information is given out to the user after every minute. It is then represented as hourly, daily, and monthly. Therefore you can easily analyze the information after every minute and compare the trend of the stock in the price and in the traded volumes. All the actions are therefore represented on the chart such that every time a transaction takes place, it is recorded on the tape, giving the amount of stock traded and at what price. The curve of the chart, therefore, gives the fluctuation of the stock in value. Real-time information is useful for traders who buy or sell stock during the day. The information is useful in calculating the loss or profit expected, especially for the traders who have stayed in the same position for a long time. As the stock in the market changes hands, there will be an update on the profit and loss, thus enabling the trader to make a decision on whether to buy back the shares he or she had sold or sell the ones he has without making much loss. Real-time data is also useful to traders that are on the screen and want to react on stock news or news stories that affect the stock trade. These are investors who stay in one trading position for a long time and mostly rely on the news on the valuation of the company they hold their stock to change their position. The information is also used by daily traders who have applications that create charts that they use to monitor the movement of stock and make daily transactions. The delay in the update of real-time data can be costly to traders who rely on charts created from real-time data. Therefore, depending on you're the type of trading you prefer, daily or long term, real-time market data is useful.

NASDAQ Level 2 and Bid-Ask

The NASDAQ level 2 was a service that was introduced in stock trading to all the traders to access real-time NASDAQ order book. It gives the traders information on the depth of trading and the momentum of the market in terms of traders and investors. The traders are able to access information on price quotes made by market makers in every stock listed by NASDAQ. The information is displayed on the OTC Bulletin Board; it has a window that displays on the left side showing the prices and sizes and on the right side. Price provided on level 2 is not an actual reflection of the trade levels. The NASDAQ only provides the available price, as well as the liquidity of the stock. However, trading with the NASDAQ level 2 quotes is that the traders use the much information provided by to gauge the level of the interest of if the institutional investors in large stocks and the sizes that they are ready to trade with.

The daily market trading of stock provides different prices for traders, which are updated in real-time as long as the market is open. These prices are the bid price, the ask, and the last price. The bid is the highest price the order is currently being given for buying, while the asking price is the lowest cost that a seller is a will to sell at. The individual buying stock, therefore, looks for the bid price while the seller always looks for the asking price. The difference between the two prices is called the spread. The two prices are a very important concept, and it should not be ignored by traders; it represents the demand and supply of the stock. Looking at the market, if the stock quotation has a bid of $13 and an ask equivalent to $13.20, a buyer will buy the stock at $13.2, and the seller will sell the stock at $13.

Buy and Sell Orders

Stocks in the market are bought and sold according to the orders given by the seller or the buyer. One of the orders is the market order, which is an order given by the one selling or purchasing the stock to sell or purchase the stock according to the best market price available. There is the limit order which allows the selling or purchasing of stock when the price of the stock does not pass a certain price of the stock. For example, sell the stock when the price does not fall beyond $4.50 or buy only when the price of the stock does not exceed $4.5. In this case, the buying limit is on the higher side while the selling order is on the lower side to reduce the chances of making losses in the case of selling and in the case of buying at a high price. There is also a stop order which counters the order given to buy or sell the stock. This happens when the price of the stock reaches a point where the trader feels that he or she will make losses if the already given order is executed. The order is the stop sell order if it was a selling order and stop buying order if the order being stopped is buying order. There is also the stop-limit order, which gives an order to stop the limit that was placed on the purchase or buying of stock. This order is given by the trader to give him or her a chance to control the price at which stock will be purchased or sold.

Other orders to buy or sell orders include the Good 'Til Canceled (GTC) order. There are some stocks that are only available for trading within a given time that is determined by the trader or broker, and they can only be sold or bought when it has not been canceled by the one selling or buying stock. Therefore, before acting on such an order, the trader is advised to contact the brokerage company to find out when the order will be canceled. There is also the Immediate-Or-Cancel (IOC) order, whereby the order is supposed to be executed immediately or canceled. If it is selling, it should be immediate, or they sell canceled. The All-Or-None (AON) order is an order that gives directives that the whole order must be executed in entirety, and if it is not, then none of the instructions of the order should be executed.

Hot Keys

Individual traders have to devise ways by which trades can be executed faster. One of the tools used is Hot Keys; these are commands that the individual trader uses to connect with the broker so that when he or she touches the keys, he sends an order to sell or buy stocks. The trader can also use Hot Keys to leave to enter a trade. Can you imagine that you want to leave the trade, and you use a mouse by clicking or appropriate section on the web or typing the statement that will prompt the inter-phase you are using to leave the trade? It would take a lot of time, and it might cause losses to the trader. This is useful especially to the daily traders; daily trading requires that the trader uses fast-moving stock to realize a reasonable profit, and this means that you move in and out of trades very fast.

The most crucial keys to set are the selling keys; remember that you have to place your sell order quickly to make sure that the price that you are selling is the one that you had seen before you gave the order. Any delay would mean losses set in. you can set the several keys for selling and include a limit order that allows you not to sell below a certain value below the bid. The trader can also use HotKeys to change the route of the trade such that if you feel that a certain route is not giving you a good offer, you quickly change to another route using a HotKey. You can also set keys for canceling open orders whenever you want to and for selling orders that are on "ask command. When you have all these keys and many others, you know that you will always act in time to avoid losses and maximize profits.

Watch List and Scanners

In stock trading, everyone always wants to get a better deal, and they always have the type of deal they want to make a profit. Your wish deal cannot just find you on the screen of your computer, and therefore, there is a need to use tools that can help you to get your wish deal. Such tools include stock scanners; these are tools that search and screen the market to find stocks that fit your description.

The buyer or the seller, therefore, feeds the set of criteria he or she wants for trading on the scanner and gives the command to search. If the trader is not satisfied with the results of the scanner, he or she can modify the search criteria to find a desirable partner for trade.

The criteria for getting the best scan results include parameters in terms of prices, the volume traded in a day, the stock exchange market. This is to avoid getting stock that is not liquid and penny stocks. Use a quality search and not quantity; the scanner should be selective enough to give the trader better results that meet his or her criteria. The scanner should also give the trader stock that has a significant price movement. This means that there must be frequent changes in the price of the stock; such a characteristic assures the trader that he or she can easily sell the stock to get back the invested funds. The scanner should also be discriminating in terms of the segments of the market; the scanner should be able to give the trader results within the segment that he or she acquainted with. A new segment requires that the trader takes time to know the market before placing any trade.

At any given time, there are thousands of stocks being traded, but not all the stocks present an opportunity for trade. It is, therefore, good to keep a watch list for when you sense that they have the potential to become an opportunity for trade. For example, there is a time when stock in the banking area consistently shows the potential to welcome a trade on your side; for constant monitoring, it is good to put the stocks in the banking sector on a watch list. Watch lists assist the trader in keeping tabs that show a collection of stocks that you quickly want to access and monitor their trading trend. Stock scanners can be used to find a good watch list. As the scanner search for stocks, they easily access new markets and introduce you to new stocks. You can now put the stocks on the watch list for monitoring.

Trading Communities

The stock trading, like any other trading institution, has joined a group known as community trading. It is a group of traders in stock who have come together to discuss issues affecting their business. When you are a member of this community, there are benefits that you enjoy, which include connecting traders and provides an environment that is comfortable for all the traders. With this community, it is easier to find a trader that matches your description of trade in terms of the number of stocks and the pricing of the stock. The traders in the community are labeled according to the experience they have in the community and the stock trading business. Therefore, the community can act as the best place to get reputable brokerage companies and individuals. Members of this community adhere to the rules of professional trading, which gives traders that are members to trade without fear of exploitation.

The community is made up of former traders, private and public company traders, and individual traders who give professional advice. These traders have enough experience both in the past and present. Also, because all the sectors in the economy are represented, there is a possibility that the advice given is well thought out and based on experience and real-time information. This advice can be used to make decisions in trades and make plans for future investments. They also have programs that educate its members in the new ventures, how to recognize trends and plan for the investment, among other programs; there is no doubt that you will grow when you are a member of this community.

There is also sharing of information on the analysis of market trades, charts that are used to make a decision on trade, plans of the market to improve trading, important trading ideas, and reviews of previous trades, among others. It is a real community where there is real interaction on issues affecting the trade positively and negatively, and therefore, discussions are held, and feedback responded to make everyone satisfied. With the advancement in technology, the trading community has become more accessible to any trader who wants to join, as most of the engagement is done online, just like in the trading. The technology also allows the members to get major breaking news that affects the stock trading industry, which helps to make a timely decision in trades and investment. As a stock trader, choose a trading community within your segment and join to enjoy the benefits like other traders.

Chapter 5: Introduction to Candlesticks

Price Action and Mass Psychology

Price action is the motion of a security price that is planned over a period of time. Price action is the starting point of all the trading analysis charts. For short term traders, price action is very important for them as it helps them make trading decisions. For technical analysis, price in action is very important as an observation of the movement of the past prices helps in calculating and advising trading decisions.

Mass psychology is what determines the changes in price action. It is when the buyers and sellers reach a consensus that continually affects the differences in prices of the trading market. This mass behavior, when traders seem to make the same decision in the trade for safety measures, is what is called mass psychology. Mass psychology cannot be influenced, but studying it and understanding it helps traders make various marketing decisions depending on the market situation. People usually make trading decisions based on how many people are making the same decision. This is somehow copying where traders feel safe, making a trade that involves many people rather than taking the risk to create a unique trade decision. Everyone, whether trading or not, believes that where a large group of people is involved, there is less likely to a lot of risks involved. It works to a certain extent, as long as the prices move along the predicted direction. But a small change in the direction could bring complete havoc for the traders.

New traders will enter into the trading market when there is a big lead on the direction of the trade; it even seems like a trend. This is eye-catching, and the trader will think to themselves to follow the trend thinking that's where the profits are. But when the new trader enters the market, several things may happen that will change the trend. Some traders may want out so that they make big profits because, at that point, the market has made them large profits. Other traders may start to have doubts about the trend and for fear of losses opt-out as well. This is very risky for a trader who joined the trend, thinking that they are safe because the market seems established. It is for this reason why it is very important to study the mass psychology so that as a trader you are aware of these risks. It is also very important that traders keep in check of what is happening in terms of current affairs because small unexpected information may be passed that could result in enormous changes in the market. At these times of change, traders are advised to keep away from entering the market. Most times, big news does not affect the short-term moves as there is already a prediction of the move happening.

It is, therefore, important for short-term or long- term to learn about the market. Learning how the price action works and learning how to predict it as a trader. Following the mass is dangerous because everyone might wake up the next morning and decide to opt-out or change the direction. It may be favorable for a trader who has the advantage of changing earlier in the market. But for a trader who reactivates later when he has been trading for long following the trend, it may cost him a lot of money. Reactivating is a great advantage to the trading market, but it is not as easy as just opting from one trend into another. A good market analysis is required so that a trader may make wise decisions. Instead of following the masses, analyzing the market for a trader is much more dependable.

Bullish Candlesticks

A bullish candlestick is also called the hollow candlestick. It's white, and it indicates that the closing price in the trading market was more significant than what was the opening price. It shows how the buying pressure of the market at the end of the day was. Both ends of the candlestick are known as shadows, and they indicate how the day's prices ranged from the low to high. The top end of the candlestick indicates the highest price while the bottom end of the candlestick indicates the lowest price experienced during the day.

As time goes by, the daily formation of group candlestick begins to form a pattern. The pattern is easily seen at around one month as more and more candlesticks will start to form into groups. This is important because it becomes easier for traders to make better price predictions for the market. The pattern works best because it shows how the price range is moving. And in case a trader wants a reactivation, this is the best way to find out on time when to reactivate. The pattern may start showing earlier than the four weeks, but it is said to be a weak pattern because anything can change any time.

Bullish reversal patterns are only formed after there has been a downtrend in the market. Without the downtrend, the formation is continuous and, therefore, not a reverse pattern. Three days into the reverse pattern, bullish confirmation is formed. This means that within the three days, there is an upside price motion, which is indicated by a tall hollow candlestick. This formation usually indicates that there has been excess trading in the market.

There are various ways to determine the daily buying pressure, which are traditional ways of technical analysis. Different candlestick patterns notify a trader when it's time to buy.

The Hammer or inverted Hammer

The hammer is a reversal pattern that alerts traders when a stock is about to reach the bottom downtrend. The candlestick in this is usually short, but the shadow to it is longer, this shows that the sellers are influencing the prices to go down during the trade. However, right before the close of the day, the buying pressure will be stronger and cause a high close. This is not to mean that the upward movement should be ignored; it is very important to keep a check on it before making a conclusion.

The inverted hammer is also a downtrend indicator. It is similar to the hammer, but it has a long shadow at the top. The long shadow at the top shows the buying pressure after the opening price has been indicated. The selling pressure will try to take over but will be insufficient to make the price go lower after the opening price had been marked.

The bullish patterns are continuous, meaning that stock will either move up, make a diversion then go up again. Then there is the bullish engulfing pattern, which is a two-line pattern. The white candlestick second line overtakes the black candlestick first line. The pattern in this also happens in a downtrend to indicate its reversal. When the trading volume takes over the second line, then the pattern is more dependable. An observation of the after candles is important for the bullish engulfing pattern. Confirmation is very important in all the patterns because it may call out for urgent reactivation from the trader. The appearance of the bullish engulfing trend is very crucial from the trading chart. The candlestick pattern is usually short-termed, and the market goes down further. This is even more possible if there is strong resistance on top of the bullish engulfing pattern. When an engulfing bulling pattern is confirmed, then the second line usually makes a supporting section.

Bearish Candlesticks

Bearish candlesticks alert a trader when the selling power is about to begin. The trading market is a battlefield between the buyers and the sellers. At the end of each day, one side has to take over. The bearish candlestick represents the sellers, while the bullish candlestick represents the buyers. This is mostly called the bear and bullfight.

When the price in the market appears to be going lower, this is an indication that the bearish is taking over. The bearish candlesticks are observed in different patterns, and their sizes vary as well. These different variations serve the purpose of giving clues on how the future market is going to be. It is for this reason of wanting to predict the future market why learning the patterns is very important. Every single candlestick shows a different movement of the price motion during the day trade. They candlesticks usually show the price movement in terms of the opening and closing prices and also the day's highs and lows. To determine the opening price and the closing price, the candlestick colors will be observed.

The closing price of the bearish candlesticks is lower. The filled part of the candlestick is what determines the real body. When the real body is short, it indicates that the market is in an indecisive state. The lines at the top of the candlesticks are called wicks, while the lines at the bottom of the candlesticks are called the tails. Generally, they are called the shadows. The top edge of the candlestick indicates the high of the day while the bottom line indicates the low of the day.

Bearing candlestick indicates that the selling pressure has just begun or is about to start. Therefore, the formation of the bearish candlestick will see the market price go down. This leads to the closing price getting lower than the opening price.

Bearish Patterns

The bearish pattern form after some weeks of observation, and they may form ranging from one to four weeks. The patterns are very important as they help predict the future movement of stocks. The patterns may either have a continuation or reversal pattern. Therefore keeping observation on this is very important as it helps determine the direction the patterns are taking. Keeping an eye on the pattern changes helps a trader informed and, therefore, easy to make buying decisions.

The bearish reversal pattern is called the head and shoulders pattern. The bearish reversal pattern has both the left and right shoulders plus the neck. The neck acts as the stock support, and in case the support is broken by the stock, then there is a downtrend in the market. All informed traders are aware of the importance of waiting for a reversal confirmation before deciding on buying. Failure to this, a trader may make a decision that may cost him so much. Patterns always form on the stock charts and are unpredictable because they can change at any time.

For technical analysis, using bearish candlestick is important as candlesticks give different signals. And from the many signals given by the candlesticks, only one is the support and the other acts as resistance. What this means is that if you miss one signal or mistake it for the other, it could significantly affect you as a trader. What makes a successful trader is the ability to find these two major signals, the support and resistance. This is assisted by the top line and the bottom lines in candlesticks. Therefore for any trader to be successful, it is essential to keep observing the signals instead of relying on news predictions. Numerous experts in trading can help beginners to avoid significant risks.

Indecision Candlesticks

An indecision candlestick means that it is a candlestick that does not follow any pattern. This means that it does not predict the market the way the bullish and bearish do. The indecision candlestick pattern is most likely to occur during the support or resistance phase. What this indicates, therefore, is that the market remained constant. Usually, one side of either the buyers or the sellers is supposed to carry the day. During indecision candlestick, however, it means that neither carried the day.

This is mainly the reason why traders are advised to keep checking on the trade patterns so that they are able to keep off from indecisive price situations in the market. Great market observations will help identify this. It is also great for traders to take all the trading ideas into considerations without underestimating any. Recognizing what to go for in the market and also being aware of what to keep away from is what matters to help avoid an indecisive candlestick situation. A trader should get to know how much the risk they are about to take will cost them as well as how not taking the risk would cost them.

The best way to observe the indecision candlesticks is by observing the charts. When short candlesticks with long wicks appear from the two sides, this is a clear indication of an indecisive candlestick. The price action is not making any directions, and it is therefore advisable that traders keep off from trading until there is a sign of the market strengths.

What indecision candlestick means on a personal level for the trader is that they have allowed some market errors of observation. A wiser trader will keep off the market instantly without having to wait and watch whether things will get back to the norm. Waiting may make the market situation worse that is why it is not very wise to play with indecision candlesticks. Therefore it is a great idea only to stick and commit to signals that provide clear decisions like the bullish and the bearish. The best way to avoid this situation is by keeping a daily observation on the charts. It may seem like too much work, but it pays off.

It is possible to make changes in the market by fine-tuning when you foresee a problem, but it needs a very experienced person to make it possible. It requires a lot of mastering of the charts because fine-tuning involves a short period of time, in between the hours. For a person who has not mastered this art, it is futile because the trade will close before they have made any movement. Time is very important for traders; in the long run, taking each trading day at a time will ensure that in the long learning, one can easily read the signals and avoid being in an indecisive candlestick situation.

Reducing the number of trade setup per week is very important as it helps a trader keep the focus on that particular setup. If a trader focused on several setups, they are unlike to make more profits as compared to sticking to just one. Being a good trader is not determined by the many setups one can take; what matters is the results seen in profits at the end of the trading month. One set up as many people argue is very risky, but it is also very important to do this. If a person concentrates on just one setup, they are most likely to make more profits than someone who is doing several trades. Many people opt for several trades because they think it gives them a lot of profits. It may be true, but many setups are complicated to observe; therefore, an indecision candlestick may hit them more than a person dealing with just one setup.

Candlestick Patterns

Candlestick patterns are technical tools that combine collected data from different periods of time and help decide on the price. Good candlestick patterns have the ability to produce great profits for both short term and long term traders. Candlesticks are significant determinants of the price movements and rates. Each candlestick predicts the prices as either high or low, and also anticipates the duration. However, they can only predict the period depending on the set limits of the chart in question, which is either on a daily, weekly, or monthly basis. Candlesticks follow either the continuation pattern or the reversal patterns. The reversal candlesticks foretell any changes in the price movement while the continuation patterns predict the continuous flow of the current prices in the same direction.

White candlesticks indicate that the closing is higher than the opening. A black candlestick, on the other hand, will indicate that the closing is lower than the opening.

Three Line Strike

It is also called the bullish three line strike reversal pattern. It shows three lines that are black in color and indicate a price downtrend.

What happens is that the three bars trade at the low range and still closes at lower near the intra-bar. Then the fourth bar that follows the three goes even more lowly but eventually manages to close high at the beginning of the three candles. This reversal foretells enormous profits for the traders.

Two Black Gapping

This is a bearish continuation pattern that has two black gapping. It shows up in the charts after there has been a continuous uptrend with a gap that shoots downwards, making the two black lines post even low prices. This pattern foretells that there will be further decline that will lead to an even more significant decrease, which results in very low prices.

Three Black Crows

This is a bearish reversal pattern that begins at the very top of an uptrend. The three bars form lows next to the intra-bar lows. This foretells a decline will continue on the lows that may lead to a big downtrend. It, therefore, predicts low prices lower than the two black gapping.

Evening Star

This pattern is bearish and starts with a very long white bar that takes an uptrend even higher than it was. It goes higher even on the bars near it, but no new traders are willing to buy, and therefore, it leads to very little range. When there is a gap in the third bar, the pattern then starts to the point that there will be a downtrend that will result in even lower lows. This is a downtrend prediction.

Abandoned Baby

This is a bullish reversal pattern that appears at the very bottom of a downtrend after a number of black candles have established the lows. There is a further gap in the next bar, but there are still no new willing traders to sell. Therefore this will lead to a closure in the market with the same closing price as was in the opening price. This foretells some good news to the traders that there will be some sort of market stabilization to very big highs.

The Bottom Line

This pattern focuses on the market but is not always dependable because it ignores a lot of signals. IT, therefore, calls for careful pattern selection, and this is only possible if traders can buy and sell signals. This, therefore, calls for a lot of research so that a trader can select the best candlestick. Ignoring the reversal and continuation signals is very dangerous for a trader as it can pose potential loses. To avoid this, however, some traders opt to buy accounts that will help read all the signals.

Chapter 6: Important Day Trading Strategies

Position Sizing and Trade Management

Trade management refers to the activities a trader engages in after the action of trade has been consummated. In a bid to create a counter for the risks whenever they happen. At the onset of the consummation, traders involved in the trade will speak in order to formulate a management plan. Position sizing, on the other hand, refers to the magnitude of a position within a specific portfolio. The amount of units that have been invested by a particular investor is his or her position size. When you are gauging an individual's position size, there are a number of factors that need to be put into consideration. The amount in dollars of what a trader is going to trade has also been referred to as the trader's position size.

With position size, there are a number of factors that need to into consideration. You have to determine the account risk. When determining the account risk, it is said that the initial process before a trader employs any use of position sizing, they have to look into their account risk. This is the capital input of a particular investor in a particular subject. Research has it that most investors risk no more than two percent of the capital in which they have invested in any specific trade. The investor being the sole controller of the capital, he or she must be in a position to know when the business is on a downward graph and make adjustments in order to change this. The investor also needs to be in a position to look on to the determination of proper position size. In order to achieve this, the investor needs to work out the account risk against the trade risk.

Strategy 1: ABCD Pattern

This refers to the common movement in which the market adopts. There are various trends in which the market adopts. There is a common style that rhymes, which have been popular over the recent past. The pattern reflects on various aspects. These aspects include time and price. The ABCD pattern is a pattern whereby all the other patterns derive from it. This kind of pattern is made up of three price swings. The variables CD and AB are straight lines called legs. The line BC is known as a retracement. This is also known as a correction.

There is a type of ABCD pattern that is known as a bullish. This type of pattern follows a trend that is focused on the down — the reversal of this, which is most of the time not likely to happen. When there is an uptrend, the potential existence of the reversal of this, then the bullish trend is formed. When trading in both bullish and bearish, the rules tend to cut across. The ABCD pattern has several types, which include: The classic one, the AB=CD Pattern, and the third type. The point of entry of this particular type of trade is when the trade has reached point D. When trading in bullish, the C has to be lower than A, and when the price rises after B, C has to be high that follows B.

It should be noted that when the market is almost at the place where D is supposed to be found, one should not be in a hurry to go trading. Through the use of various methods, one can see to it that the price of the commodity has been reverse to where it was. When you encompass resistance and support, you are able to achieve effective use of these resources.

Strategy 2: Bull Flag Momentum

When a stock is in a complete uptrend, is when this type of pattern occurs. Its representation on the chart is in the form of a flag pole and thus the name. Considering the fact that the trend is on the rise, then this type of flag is referred to as the bullish flag. The characteristics of this bullish flag include: The stock is forming a strong rise in the volume relativity and thus forming the pole. The stock arranges itself at the top of the pole; thus, the resulting effect is the formation of a flag. After the consolidation pattern has been achieved, the stock comes out of it once more in order for it to maintain its upward trend.

With Bull flags, the time strategy is wide enough to accommodate any structure. Bull flags work best in a short-term time frame and are effective too. Most of the time, they are used on a five to two-minute time frame. However, on a day to day basis, these bull flags are effective too. When trading in Bull flags, the procedure is less subtle. The tricky part comes when you are looking for them. The major thing to search for in this particular pattern is the volume at hand; the volume is a key point when it comes to this particular pattern. A defined trading line that is on the fall is another thing that you need to search for. The advantage of bull flags is that they have an edge of statistics when they are traded in the same manner. When you place a stop below the area of consolidation, this is one way in which you are managing this particular type of trade.

Strategy 3 & 4: Reversal Trading

Reverse trading refers to the act of trade that suggests affecting the position of an investor back to the starting point. Reverse trading ca entail the acquiring of an index contract of stock that has been previously short sold. This is what is known as reverse trading. When trading, there is an expected futuristic position that should be depicted. When this position is closed out, the trade is said to have been reversed. A reversal, on the other hand, refers to the change in price or the direction of an asset. Depending on the prevailing circumstances, the reversal that happens could be on the downside or the upside.

With reversals, they are keen to note the overall direction of the price and not based on merely based on periods. In order to spot reversals, there are some key pointers that ought to be used. These pointers include trend lines or moving averages. A reversal is an indicator of the changes in price trends. It could be that the trend has changed from an upward to a downward or vice versa. When the position of the price is underway reversal, traders will try their best to get out of the price. Large changes in the price are what is known as a reversal. Pullbacks are prone to happen in the face of changes in the price. These pullbacks happen in a bid to inhibit the direction of the price from changing.

At its onset, it is almost subtle to distinguish a pullback from a reversal. With a reversal, it will keep on going until it sees the formation of a new trend line. The difference with the pull-back comes in when the price starts changing. A pullback will ease when the price starts to change.

Strategy 5: Moving Average Trend Trading

This is a type of technical analysis that is simple in nature and is used to smooth put price data. This type of strategy seeks to create an average price. His average updated price is collected over a period of time, depending on the preferences of the trader. There are various types of advantages that come about as a result of employing this particular type of strategy in your training. This type of strategy can be customized in that it is able to fit into your specific time frame. This has both those planning to trade in the long term and in the short term. When using a moving average, the procedure is less subtle since you are able to observe the movements by yourself. For instance, when the angle is facing up, it suggests that the price is in an upward movement. When it is facing down, it suggests that the price is also moving down. When it is moving sideways, then the price is on average. A moving average may also be used as a resistance or support. When in an uptrend, between a 50 day and a 200-day moving average may be used as a support. This is because it provides a basis for the floor. This is because the price will bounce off it. When in a downtrend, the moving average can be used as a resistance whereby the price will get to this level and then start to fall again.

It is normal for the price to go out of its way. The movement of the moving average may not always follow the same trend and may change according to circumstances. When the price is above the moving average, then you can deduce that the scheme is up when it is below the moving average, you can deduce that the scheme is on a low.

Strategy 6: VWAP Trading

From the wording of it, VWAP refers to the Volume Weighted Average Price. This type of trading gives the mean price in which a security has engaged in trading in the course of the day. The elements of volume and price are dominant. Traders are provided with information about volume and price. Hey, we are thus aware of the trend and how particular security is valued. Every dollar traded in every transaction is added up in a bid to calculate VWAP. This amount is then multiplied by the number of shares traded and then put against the number of shares traded.

This type of strategy is used by various institutional buyers when they seek to leave or get into various stocks without creating a large impact. The price is reset to average when various institutions buy when the price is below the VWAP and in turn, sell when it is above it. When retailers use this type of strategy, it acts as if I a moving trend, and it helps to confirm the various trends that seem to be in existence. VWAP and moving average can be linked to each other in the manner that one may think they are one and the same. This is not the case as VWAP entails calculating the price by multiplying by volume and dividing by total volume. The case with moving prices is different as it entails the calculation of adding up closing prices that have accumulated over a certain period of time; it could be ten weeks. With VWAP, this is a single day trading indicator that is closed at the end of one day and then restarted at the beginning of the next day.

Strategy 7: Support or Resistance Trading

These are points in the trading curve where it is anticipated that the price will stop and start to reverse. With these prices, there is a demotion of touching on the price, although there is no breakthrough in the particular price. As the price falls, it will stop at some point when it finds its basis. This is the floor, and it is referred to as the support. The price here will not breakthrough but rather bounce off the floor of support. If it passes this first support, it is likely to continue with the same trend until it reaches another support level. The opposite of support is resistance. With resistance, the price is rising. As the price rises, there are a number of factors that will bring about friction. This is what is referred to as resistance. When the price reaches the resistance level, it is likely to bounce back and start falling. There are some instances where this might not be the case as the price may breakthrough. When this happens. The trend is followed until another resistance level is reached.

When the support and resistance levels are predictable, they are said to be pro-active. They operate on a speculative nature in that they cite areas when the price has not been. There focus is often on the actions of the current price. There is another form of support and resistance method known as reactive. This type of support and trading occur as a result of volume behavior and price action. Trend lines are the yardsticks that are used in a bid to identify support and resistance levels. If a price gets through a support level, then that support level becomes resistance. The vice versa is also true.

Strategy 8: Red to Green Trading

Moving from red to green in reference to price entails that the price moves from below the amount of the previous close to above the amount of the previous close. Trading below the stock that closed the previous day is considered as red, whereas trading above the stock that closed the previous day is considered as green. There is a shift in momentum when a price navigates from red to green. With this kind of shift in place, one is able to anticipate risk. The stock gains its volatility often at this time. This comes in handy when creating day to day setups for.

When deciding to make this move from red to green, there are a number of factors that you need to look for. Volume is key. The volume of your stock must directly relate to the buyers at hand. There are a number of instances, however, where an individual may buy on the green and sell on the red. This often means that you have bought above the stock that closed the previous day and sold below its closing stock of the previous day. The purchase of stock, however, should be only when you have started to grow in your business. The green is often an indicator that you can buy stock. To most people, bargaining is mostly subtle, and thus, as a result, they tend to shy away from it. These types of people rush into buying stock without properly gauging them properly. You buy a property, for instance, that is decreasing in value. In order to invest properly, you need to go with the trend. In the day to day, trading failing to follow the trend is an act of contempt that can be linked to swimming upstream.

Strategy 9: Opening Range Breakouts

The opening range is one of the most versatile periods of day-trading. This is because it is key to day trading. The period after a market opens, there are often highs and lows, which can be referred to as opening range. The period ranges from twenty to thirty minutes of trading in the first trading hour. The topsy-turvy during this period is that you want to identify the periods of lows and highs in the market as well as account for the same. This is because both these factors are connected in a manner that is more direct. This opening period is characterized by big volumes of trade. In a nutshell, opening ranges are used as entry points to the market and also as forecast to the trading of the day.

In order to benefit from the opening range, you need to first account for its size. There is a popular strategy known as the Early Morning Range Break out. This type of strategy works in a bid to identify the gaps available. When we have the identity of the gap, we have to focus on the direction of the breakout. Later in the day, when you will be approaching breakouts, you need to do this with extra-caution. In order to make sure that you stay in the gap, you need to use the minimum price in relation to the gap. The pullback gap strategy is also another strategy that has been used. This type of strategy works in a bid to predict when the pullback will diminish. Gap reversal has also been used. This is the process when the price is used to create a gap. When the price is bullish, there is a gap reversal when the price breaks.

Other trading Strategies

Apart from the aforementioned strategies of trading, there exist other types of trading strategies which include:

Position Trading

This is a type of trading strategy that focuses its radar on long-term trading and the price movement. The main movements in prices result in gaining large amounts of profits. This type of strategy is one that is long-term in nature, and that fails to thrive on a day to day basis. Traders who engage in this type of trade analyses the market for weeks and even months before they can engage in any trade. These types of traders will not be concerned by the shifts in price that are minor.

Swing Trading

This is another type of trading strategy that entails holding positions for quite some time. When engaging in swing trading, traders would hold market positions for quite some time in order to thrive when there is some short term shift in the market. This particular type of trading strategy has been seen to go hand in hand with individuals who engage in other forms of the profession. Swing trading encompasses other strategies say trend trading, break out trading, and momentum trading.

Break out Trading

In order to understand what break out trading is, we need to first establish what a break out is. A break out is a price that heading to the outer limits of a resistance and support level. This type of trading is used by people who are investing actively. This strategy happens to be where most of the prices start from. When this strategy is managed properly, it can offer a downside risk that is limited. With the break out trading, you will find that a trader engages in a long position. This is after the price has broken above resistance and has entered a short position.

Developing Your Own Strategy

You are an active business person who has been constantly engaging in trading. Most of the trading strategies do not work for you. In order to design your own trading strategy, there are a number of factors that you need to put in place. These are:

Having a background set of information about the decision that you are about to engage in is key. You need to first understand where you are before you can know where you are heading to. This is done by having a view of where you are, your past performances. The business is made up of various facets, and in order to achieve maximum analysis, you need to look at each fact vis a vis its performance. Focus on your efforts and shortcomings. In order to capitalize on this, you need to maximize your strengths. When you are seeking in-depth information, it is key to take note of the various sources of information that you may engage in. The right kind of expert advice will take you places.

With a vision statement, you are in a position to determine the future direction of the business. This will act as a motivating factor towards what you want to achieve. Your vision should work hand in hand with your mission. What should follow this is the identification of the strategic. With the strategies in place, you ought to deliver a tactical plan. The tactical plans mean that you are making the strategies come to life. These are actions directed towards various areas that you ha earlier highlighted. Focusing on your weaknesses will make sure that you are taking risk measures to curb any risk of arises. With this in place, you can now implement your plans.

Trading Based on the time of the day

When trading on a day to day basis, most of the time, you live your life with your heart in the hands. This is because, by the pass of every second or hour, major changes in the market occur, which often have big implications. Most of the time, the ordinary course of business ensues. Depending on the time zone that you are in, day trading will always commence very early in the morning; thus, it may work in favor of early risers.

There are a number of hours which are specific for trading. These types of trading hours are key because it is only in these hours that you are able to maximize your efforts. Trading in the day is a dirty expedition because even the most experienced traders tend to result in losses. With day trading, one requires a heightened amount of focus and discipline. Trading during the opening has a lot of implications. Trading at the open means that you are trading one or two hours after the stock has opened. The most volatile time of the market is the time when the opportunity hits the most. There is often a large number of people who are investing at this time. Most of them are doing this for the first time and do not have a pre-perception of the market. When a trader is new in the market, he or she is advised not to engage in trade in the first fifteen minutes when the day opens. In this time period, the biggest trades in the trend have been seen to be exhibited.

Trading would regularly begin at 0930 hours and end at 1030 hours. This is often the period of the day when it is favorable for people to engage in trade. The session `can then be extended for one hour to 1130 hours. It is key to note that before engaging in day trading, you need to have a candid understanding of the market because even professional traders have failed to thrive at these moments. People should not depend on the advertisement in Televisions and on radio stations in order to make decisions on day trading. When information hits advertisements, this is potentially old news. When trading with this type of information, it can affect the movement of price in one direction. This then results in a loss. The motive of engaging in any business is to gain profit.

Chapter 7: Step by Step to a Successful Trade

In life, everyone has the drive and urge to being the best and successful in everything that they do in their daily lives. Someone would give his or her all to what they do to get noticed and more so be successful in the long run. Success does not come easy as it might look like. There are various sacrifices and attributes that one requires in order to be successful. Day trading is not an exception, as it also requires some sense of discipline and step by step strategies that will make it successful. With these strategies in place, the trade would then be able to maximize profits and do away with any losses. At this point, we can then term the trade as successful. We are going to, therefore, dwell on the step by step process of a successful trade.

Building a Watchlist

A watchlist is a very vital tool in a trade that is used in monitoring all the trade or business activities. It is also used in planning the future of your investment in a certain market. A watchlist will help you as a trader to have the list of all stock which can readily be dealt with in different markets, thus making you advantageous in terms of competition in the market. The watch list will also give you an upper hand in monitoring the criteria which you might be looking for and thus know how to employ it fully.

Before building a watchlist, you should first be able to differentiate between a watchlist and a portfolio. The fact that a portfolio usually gives the list of only owned stock makes it different from a watchlist. On the other hand, a watchlist usually shows the securities you own together with those which you have selected even if you have not ventured into the trade. Therefore, a watchlist will give you a hint of the kind of stock that you may find necessary in your portfolio. A portfolio should thus be built wisely to ensure that the best is made out of it and in the long run, a successful trade. The following are a few tips that can be put in practice to ensure that you come up with an efficient watchlist:

Keep It Fresh and Simple

When focused on having a successful day trader, it means that you should be able to do various researches on the market. In case you have watchlists which you made from the previous researches, then they are very vital in finding the fine-tuning of your futures day trade. As much as the previous watchlists are important and act as reminders, you should also come up with a watchlist that is based on the present market factors. This will ensure that the trade you are venturing into complies with the current market directives and policies.

Different people usually have different criteria and approaches to their trade plans. It is, therefore, very important to always go through your watchlist in order to determine whether it is still matching the criteria that you had earlier set. In case, the watchlist is no longer in harmony with your criteria, then you will be required to do away with the stock and now have the stock that complies with the current market trends and policies. In this way, you will avoid being overwhelmed by a long list of the stocks, which some no longer fit into your criteria. In this way, you will be able to have full control easily and focus on your day trading, thus come up with a perfect watchlist that will guide you achieve a successful trade.

Look for What You Need

When in the process of building a watchlist, it is very important to scan both prospective and existing markets discretely. This is meant to determine the specific and distinctive criteria that you are in search of. In this case, there are various factors that you should consider having in mind that the preferences that you have are capable of fluctuating with time. You should, therefore, filter your preferences by the criteria you set one at a time. This will enable you to come up with a very detailed watchlist that will help you be a successful day trader.

When scanning the market, there are various rules and guidelines that you have to comply with fully. These rules include;

- You should analyze the patterns which indicate either lower or higher trend changes in the market.
- The daily percentage change in market trends, more specifically when the volume of daily stocks is greater than average, meaning that they will have hit 52-week lows or highs.
- Signals which measures trends that are unusual. These trends include a relatively low deviation of prices with an increase in the daily volume.

Having complied with these rules, then you will be able to efficiently and much easily scan the market. In the end, you will come up with a perfect watch list that will help you be a successful day trader.

Always Be Informed About the Market

Building a watchlist that is efficient requires you to have knowledge of the trends and changes taking place in the stock market and its environs. This knowledge usually comes from a learning experience that is procedural. Having acquired this knowledge, then you shall realize that the rewards and achievements will be worth it. This will entail you familiarizing yourself with the way in which the changing capitalization levels directly affect the various sectors in the market.

When coming up with a watchlist, economic cycles are usually very vital, and they are usually time-consuming to analyze. Despite being time-consuming, this information is very critical, as it is one of the factors that will enable you to come up with a comprehensive and detailed watchlist. With time, you will be able to come up with your own style of day trading and thus be comfortable in the assessment of the market trends of the stocks which are in your watchlist. In this way, you shall have settled on a certain strategy, thus getting conversant with trends. In the long run, you will be comfortable converting your stocks into profits. This, therefore, means that the quality of the watchlist might end up determining the success of your day trade.

Start Big, Go Small

When building a watchlist, you should maintain deductive reasoning. This means that you should be able to start by setting broader criteria. You will then narrow down the list of stock that you were in search of while watching the market trends. Having the ideal knowledge of what you are in search of, you will then be able to weed out the stocks that are matching your criteria. In the end, you will have an effective and clean watchlist that you can effectively work from.

It is a norm for the stock market to always reinvent itself. This, therefore, requires you to also constantly change your wish list to suit the stock market trends. For the stocks to have in your wish list, this will depend on the security type that which you have decided to trade-in. apart from that, the strategies that you also have set will tend to affect your decision on the stock. It is advisable to keep your focus from the word go and also keep in mind that while getting started, it is very vital to narrow down. Following these criteria, when building your watchlist, would, therefore, mean that you will have an effective watchlist that will enable you to be successful in the day trade.

Focus on the Favorites

It is always advisable to focus on stocks that are currently popular in the market when building your watchlist. This will enable you to understand the reason why popular picks are as popular as they are. This is beyond doubt that these issues would be popular among other individuals. In the course of popularity, then they will be setting a platform for you to keep an eye on the changes in trends in the market. With this market information, you will be able to make a decision on the kind of stocks to include n your watch list.

With time learning and gathering as much information about the day trade market as possible, you will have specific big trade companies to watch. Apart from that, you will have also determined the kind of stock that is suitable for your day trade prospect and criteria to add to your watchlist. This will create a room for you to grow and dream bigger with respect to your day trade. Definitely, you will have come up with a perfect watchlist in the long run that will aid you in achieving success in your day trading venture.

Setting a Trading Plan (Entry, Exit and Stop Loss)

In any business setting since the olden time, it has been a rule that if you fail to make a plan, then you will be planning to fail. Some will say that this is just saying, but those who are serious with trading and have a goal of someday being successful will take it as a serious saying. A trader who has been in the market for long and has been successful will advise that it is your choice to either strictly stick to your written trading plan or never have a taste of success. If you have a trading plan, then it should be a detailed and objective oriented one. Failure to look into this will make the plan useless, but you have a chance of reviewing it to make it worthy in the long run.

Setting up a trading plan has got various essentials that will see it important and practical when being executed. These essentials are meant to aid you in setting up a trading plan which will guide you through the trading and possibly make you a successful trader. The following are some of the essentials necessary for setting up a trading plan:

Setting Entry Rules

The entry rules of a trading organization or business should be very complicated so as to make the trading system very effective and at the same time, ease the process of decision making. The rules should also not be many and subjective as many will tend to shy away from them, and you will fail to make trades. These conditions should, therefore, be a reasonable amount and not subjective as such so that people can be comfortable making trade, which translates to a successful trade.

This tends to explain and justify the reason why many people today prefer trading using computers. Computers are usually good at trading as compared to people. This is because computers have got no feelings and are dumb; thus, they will not necessarily need to have certain thoughts or feelings in order to trade. The computer is just set with the conditions for trading; thus, if you meet the minimum conditions, you will enter the trade. On the contrary, failure to meet the conditions means that you cannot negotiate with the computer; thus, you will be limited to trading. If you trade and it all goes wrong, or you get a profit, you can freely exit. It is, therefore, very essential to set reasonable trade entry rules in order to effectively manage the trade and be successful.

Setting Exit Rules

As compared to entry rules, any serious trader determined to succeed always handles exit rules as the most important. A majority of traders usually focuses on buying signals and ignores where and when to exit.

This even makes some traders fail to make sales when down because they fear to make losses. Professional traders usually focus on exits and even tend to lose many trades compared to those which they win. Surprisingly, they still make profits because they are good at limiting losses and managing funds. The virtue that they have good management skills when it comes to funds is because they are flexible in exiting trades at any moment.

Before entering any trade, you should first have the knowledge of where exits are. There is usually a minimum of two exits for any given trade. You should also determine your stop loss just in case the trade does not go your own way. These stop losses should be written as mental stops usually do not count. Apart from that, each and every trade should have reasonable and reachable profit targets. Once you gain entry to trade, you can find a breakeven by selling a section of your position in order to change your stop-loss position. With a reasonable stop loss, you can comfortably trade, provided good management, and be a successful trader.

Stop Loss

Stop refers to an order that is placed by a broker in order to either sell or buy once the stock has reached a set price. Stop-losses are meant for limiting investors in terms of their security position. If you set a stop loss of 10% that is below the stock price, then your loss will be limited to 10%. Stop-loss order has its own advantages and disadvantages. One main advantage is that it will not be necessary for you to be monitoring the performance of your stock on a daily basis. This is ideal, especially when you are undergoing certain situations that limit you from getting the time to monitor your stock's performance for a relatively long period of time.

On the other hand, the major disadvantage of stop-loss orders is that in case of a short term fluctuation in the price of a stock, the stop price could be activated. It is, therefore, very important to pick stop-loss percentages that would allow the stock to freely fluctuate and prevent as many risks of loss as possible. Setting a low stop-loss percentage for a stock that fluctuates at a relatively higher percentage will not do any good to you. This will most probably lead to loses as compared to the rate at which it can make you profits.

The guidelines for setting a stop-loss order solemnly depend on the individual's trading style. This refers to the length of the investment period that a trader chooses. A trader who is more active can prefer a 5% stop-loss order, and a long-term trader can prefer 15%. Apart from that, if you have reached your set stop-price, your stop-loss order will then change to be market orders. It will also change its price to be a much different price from your stop price. This majorly applies to move trades whose stock prices can change very fast within a very short period of time. The fact that brokers usually restrict individuals from placing their orders on specific securities is another limitation of stop loss.

Stop-loss is meant to mainly help traders to avoid losses. This is not the only function as it is also meant to lock profits, also referred to as 'trailing stop'. In this case, the stop loss is set at a certain percentage that is lower than the market price at that very moment and not the buying price. When the price of a stock fluctuates, the prices of stop-loss usually adjust also. This, therefore, means that an increase in stock, then you will have unrealized gains whereby you have no cash unless you make sales. The use of stop-loss will allow you to leave out some profits while making some capital gains at the same time.

Stop loss is very simple to use, but many traders usually fail to employ it. It can be very beneficial to any trader whether they are using it to lock profits or prevent losses. It can be even said to be a special kind of insurance policy. If used in a reasonable manner, it will be of great value, and you will easily be a successful trader.

Executing the Plan

Execution of the plan is the most important part of trading and at the same time, challenging. The main reason why it is said to be challenging is that this is where you actualize what was before just pieces of ideas. This is where you will need to convert your ideas and concepts into actions and behaviors. Once converted, then you shall have a trade to actually observe and manage. In order to effectively execute your plan and come up with a successful trade, you should possess certain traits to guide you. These traits include:

• Be Focused

Being focused is very vital as it ensures that there is clarity that is necessary for you to make sane decisions that will aid the achievement and success of your goals. Having a sharp focus will create a clear way of being successful in your trade. This is because you will not be easily drifted from your goals, which you intend to realize in your trade. It also means that you know the decisions to make at which situations thus not afraid of turning down activities that may hinder you from succeeding.

• Be Passionate

The most successful individuals in trades and any other investment are usually so passionate about whatever they do. This is because passion brings about the feeling of connectedness with your work. Being a trader with passion will, therefore, mean that you will give your all to it with the aim of achieving set goals and becoming a successful trader. With passion, you will be able to appreciate your performance and also be very proactive in your duties. Passion will definitely drive you towards your desires, which in turn will make you a successful trader.

• Invest in Competence

A competent person is one who has got skills, processes, tools, and systems that are required in performing a certain task. It is, therefore, very vital as it depicts your ability to get committed to trading and achievement of your goals. Building your competence will, therefore, give you the way in which you can execute your plans in the most effective way possible. A competent person can thus easily come up with ideas of executing their trading plans and become great successful traders.

Chapter 8: Next Step for Beginner Traders

A person who is just getting into the market has a lot to do than just setting up a business plan and getting started. Unlike other people who are experienced in the market, beginner traders still need to go through several processes to get to where they want. Trading is not like any other task that anyone can just wake up in the morning and say I want to do this and succeeds with it.

Beginner traders still have to learn the business world and understand how trading takes place, for them to know where to start from and how to handle their trade to keep everything going. They have a lot to learn from the expert trades than the information they already have at hand. When you get to the trading market, everything seems new and challenging for you. Some people even end up giving up on what they had planned and maybe started.

As a beginner, there must be something that pushed you to start up this business. You came up with an idea of trading and convinced yourself that you should get started. You even created a business plan that kept you posted on what you need to do to bring out a good and unique outcome. A business plan is needed by everyone in the trading market. It helps you in controlling your way of trade to arrive at your desired target.

A business plan execution is always the final step for traders who are old in the market and have full ideas on what they are doing and how to do their trades, including the adjustments that they need to make to achieve what they want in case of any changes that occur in the market during the time of trade. However, a beginner trader still has to go through additional steps to land where they want.

First, they need to learn the market pattern. Getting familiar with the patterns of trade in the market will give a beginner trader a little bit of an easy time carrying out their trades as they get to learn what they should expect at what time and how they should handle every situation when it comes to was never planned. They get exposed to the challenges that are faced in the trading market and how to cope up with them and remain stable.

After learning the trading patterns of the new market, they get to learn the risks involved and how they affect trade. The traders get prepared mentally on the type of risks to expect and how they can handle these risks to reduce the severity of loss that comes with each type of risk upon occurrence. This keeps the new graders focused and alert so that in case anything happens, they don't get too much affected and can rise and start again, and still record again.

They should learn survival tactics. Business involves both loss and gain. The skills and secrets that they learn when they are in the business market impacts a lot in their productivity. When you're that trader that hurries everything and refuses to accept even the little defeats, you will be lost and even find it hard to take the request that we agree and set a deal to clear within some period of time. Beginner traders must learn this at the beginning of the trading process to ensure that they get well along with the clients and maintain them.

Another important step that they must take is taking lessons on how to create and maintain a customer relationship with someone they are meeting for the first time. They learn how to deal with different customers, who to trust, and who not to trust. This helps the traders in the stock exchange, and they get to know the customer relationship beauty and how it works.

The Essentials for Day Trading

Day trading has become more of an online trade than an offline thing. This has made it so exciting as feedback is ever ready in less than a second. Who wouldn't love to get a faster response? Everyone is going for it because they find it a faster, cheaper, and more beneficial way of trading. Day traders have become so overwhelmed by the thought of day trading being an online task that you can handle it anywhere anytime. However, there are some essentials that the trade must-have for a successful day trading.

First, you will need a trading platform, that is, sophisticated software that will enable you to analyze and finish up trades on the market that is moving at a higher speed. These are the platforms that allow the traders to deliberately avoid using a stock broker's business that will imply unnecessary fees on them. They do trading their own way at pleasing savings.

Multiple monitors are also important to help in tracking the high running performance of stock everywhere. The traders should use at least two to three monitors in this process to provide the bare-boned in a way that is more presentable and easily understood. However, more monitors, like five to six, is an added advantage. Traders with more monitors experience high analytic flexibility and a faster way of trading as they are able to capture the motion of several ideas at a go.

Day trading also requires high-speed internet. It takes milliseconds to get feedback on what you are looking for. Low-speed internet is a disadvantage to day traders as it will break the records for fast internet connection, making them unreliable. This will make the traders lose more contracts than they gain, and by the end of it, the profit that would have been recorded with a higher speed internet is lost.

No one would want to wait for so long before having their task done when they know very well that they can have it done and completed at a shorter time when they take an alternative option. Therefore, as a day trader, you need a more reliable source of internet for you to reduce the loss and maximize your possible gains to record a higher savings trend.

Day traders rely hugely on the news feed. With the faster internet connection and several monitors at hand, the traders are required to use all the available assets and closely monitor the news events and key indicators to analyze the stock performance together with all the potential opportunities. If they don't capture the news trade and pay attention to the new posts concerning the trade, it is possible for them not to get the contracts that they need. All-day traders must be alert on the news feed on stocks.

Day trading also needs a high level of research skills. No profitable positions will ever hang on your screen, begging you to click and view them. If you wait to see, opportunities look for you, be prepared to be badly disappointed. You require basic research skills to help you make good use of the available opportunities and set your track of capital in the right direction. Train yourself to look keenly at all the opportunities and do not ignore anything that may give a hint when desperately searching for the available opportunities to hang on.

As a trader, you must also be very disciplined with everything. Discipline cannot be bought anywhere. What makes the difference between an ordinary and extraordinary traders is the descent but informative performance and self-control. The speedy trend of day trading has made traders who are not very successful in learning the need to maintain a cool head at all circumstances. During good times and bad times, the secret for survival is playing a low key and letting everything come the way they are.

All you need for you to be successful in day trading is knowing your market. Know when to hold on and when to let go. Don't be so excited at the sense that trading is doing so well, neither should you be in a hurry to rely on helping hands when things are tough. You might end up taking the wrong direction and losing everything that you would have gained had you been patient and positive on what you are doing.

The experience you have in the field of trade will also help to provide the discipline that you require to stay out of any danger that is awaiting. The trends in the market develop over decades, making traders who have less knowledge on day trading to miss out on the trending opportunities. Acquiring adequate knowledge in the sector of day trading before getting involved in it will be more adventurous to you, making your trade records more profitable.

Everyone would want to work with a highly informed and experienced person to improve productivity and record a stable trend in the market. No one would love to be dragged behind, so when you are starting day trading, you must be ready to convince your clients that you are exactly what they need and that you are never a disappointment. This will also keep you going since you have an idea of what you are doing and where you are headed to.

A good trading strategy is also needed for good trading records. The experience and the knowledge that a trader has is what helps in constructing a better strategy that will guide the decisions made by traders to avoid too much pressure that will kick them out of track. Here, everyone is a driver. A little delay in the brain causes an unexpected fall in the market.

Markets go with the flow of trends. They are influenced and pushed forward by the logic and analysis. The very same thought should help to establish a unique trading strategy, making maximum utilization of trade stops to reduce the losses, and developing the most unusual and rare swing trade. Have a detailed approach to the trading trend and make good use of what is available, and that works well. If something is broken, come up with the best plan of fixing it, then use it to win.

Every business needs capital, and so does day trading. Day trading is so much occupied with opening and closing positions in the circle of the day of trade. For the need to overcome the attrition of trade commission, traders require high capital to get to higher trading positions all round. With less capital, balancing ideas in the market place is almost close to impossible.

Money is the determinant of every baseline of success. You can't use less than expected to gain the maximum. You reap everything according to what you sew. For a highly profitable day trading, a good amount of capital is required, and financial management skills must be present for effective utilization of the available resources.

The advantage part of day trading is that you don't have to attend classes and dig deep to get what you want. This is so fortunate to those who did not get the opportunity to attend classes. They still have a choice of earning. Anyone can do this, but not with a lot of ease as it sounds to a rare person. For you to get started on day trading, you can go for the online courses to gather various ideas and the knowledge required for day trading.

Online courses are as much effective as the courses taken in schools, and the good news is that the online courses are sometimes more detailed than the information that school offers. You have the option of searching deeper and directly for what you want to know and leave what is not beneficial for you. There's no harm seeking for help from the online assistants. Go for what you need and equip yourself only with the relevant information but highly productive in the field of day trading.

Day trading can still be a challenge despite all the skills and knowledge that you have. It is not like gambling that you can just try anything, hoping that you will win. There's no trial and error game in day trading. It requires time, effort, and dedication, with highly detailed information on market trends.

Conclusion

Just like any other type of trade, day trading requires patience and self-control. Everyone involved has to be highly detailed about what they are doing. Anything did without clear information, and the idea always turns into a mess. Everyone needs to know what they are dealing with and what they should expect at the end. This is the only way you can trade with a peaceful mind.

We must accept that everything has a starting point. You must start somewhere and end somewhere. In between the several processes of trading, a lot of techniques are required to handle everything the right way. You must consider every single step important and pay due respect to the areas of trade. From day one, when you are new in the trading sector until the day that you will be stable and consider yourself an expert trader who is ready to win, you must have gone through several processes that are tough and challenging, and only the patient ones win.

Nothing is easy. No money comes looking for you in your comfort zone. You have to go out and stretch out your harms to grab opportunities that will lead you where you want. You must be tough enough to dig through the challenges without the fear of becoming the loser. Of course, if you are not well prepared and ready to cut across the edges, you will be kicked out of the way.

Nothing sounds as bitter as failing to reach your goal just because you gave up on the way. Face the struggle and be focused on what you want. This will keep everything flowing on the right track and easy to handle. You may see someone win big and think they got there easily, but this is where we all go wrong. We need shortcuts to everything and fail to consider the challenges that someone must have gone through to be where you see them.

In order to grow in any kind of business, you must be ready to learn. Collect every single idea about what you are doing and think of their effectiveness in your business. Maintain good ideas and anything that doesn't add value, and your business should be dropped but not forgotten. You can consult experts on how to go about something that you feel is effective, but you don't clearly understand. It is a very healthy way of growing your business. Cut off your ego and earn yourself what you deserve.

There are several risks involved in the trading market, and this must be accepted by every trader. There are several risk management strategies that they can adapt to deal with the risks and reduce their effects on trade results. Some risks can be avoided, but there are some that have to be faced and, if not well controlled, have a severe impact on the business.

What is most important in any kind of business is learning the trading strategies, having detailed knowledge about what you are dealing with, and being ready to face the challenges that come in between. No one is perfect. You might be old in the business sector, but still, you have to learn to expand on your business.

Options Trading for Beginners

Learn Strategies from the Experts on how to Day Trade Options for a Living!

David Hewitt & Andrew Peter

Table of Contents

Introduction

There is no doubt that the global economy is always experiencing alteration from time to time. The increase in the world population is gradually affecting the availability of jobs, and with millions of people not getting access to a collar job, online trading, cryptocurrencies, and options trading are some of the leading business ventures that people now show interest in. However, as the number of people who are interested in options trading keeps increasing, we have discovered that the ignorance rate is expanding. There is no other greatest limiting factor to success in whatever step you take in life than ignorance. And this truth applies to option trading. If you want to get the best result, then you've got to learn from experts who have done it before, who are doing it and don't plan to stop at it.

Options trading is an opportunity for anyone who wishes to earn without much stress, but this is only possible if you have a clear knowledge about it. With over four decades of existence, options trading recently started gathering waves. Do you know why? Many people believe it is hard and sophisticated. As a result of this belief, many investors didn't want to invest in it. However, options trading is not difficult. You only need to learn about it to get the excellent result you seek. Without the right knowledge, you risk the possibility of losing your investment. If all you pay attention to is the use of words, such as *risky* or *dangerous* by the media, you will most definitely not consider options trading.

Just before you make your conclusion on a baseless misconception by others, just note that engaging in options trading gives you access to an increased cost-efficiency. It is not as risky as equities, you have access to several strategic alternatives, and with the right tools and knowledge, options trading promises potential high percentage returns; and most importantly, it is a reliable means of making passive income. With the knowledge in this book, you are set to learn the strategies to improve your portfolio.

This book is a guide you need to gain access to the necessary information you must have before you venture into the options trading world. We have provided information on how options trading works, the very strategies you need to succeed at it, how to understand when to trade and when you should not trade, handing technical analysis, and building your wealth with risk management. We will not promise you that there are no challenges you will face while options trading, but we can assure you that with this book, you will be equipped to face the challenges. This guide is a compendium of answers to every possible question you may have about options trading.

The next investment move you need to make to start experiencing the financial freedom lifestyle you seek is to begin options trading now. It is an opportunity that is best grasped now. A good time for you to start options trading is yesterday, and the best time is now. Learn and digest the strategies and tips in this book and begin on a journey to achieve financial freedom in no time!

Chapter One: Unveiling Options

In the world of possibilities that we live in, taking hold of options trading is a great way to grasp one of the opportunities that the world really has to offer. Options trading makes it easy and possible for your money to work for you while you follow your other passions. With your money constantly at work, it is so easy for you to achieve the financial freedom and success you seek. So, what is options trading, and how does it work?

What is an Option?

An option is a contract that offers an investor the right to purchase or sell a security at a specific price with an agreement for a certain period. When you trade options, you are trading different securities such as ETFs, indices, equities, and many more. Options enjoy their value from their underlying assets, and this is why they are often referred to as *derivatives*. There is an options market where investors meet to buy and sell options. The contracts that are traded on the market are based on the securities hip in a company. Unlike a stock that gives you an ownership right of a company, option buying and selling gives you the ability to trade the obligation or potential to buy and sell the underlying stock of a company. If you own an option, you are not entitled to any dividend payments.

When you buy or sell options, you have the right to exercise the option at any period during the contract lifetime. What this means is that you don't have to exercise buying and selling of an option at the buy and sell point. This is why options are derivative securities. Being derivatives means they derive their price from another item or product, which will be the value of assets, such as securities and the market. In a way, the derivative nature of options makes them less risky than stocks. But to make this work for you, you've got to understand how to use options correctly.

As an investor, how do you use options? It is simple. When you buy options, you are gambling on the available stocks to either go up or down or, let me say; you are hedging a trading position in the market. So, the agreed rate you pay for the underlying asset through the option is the *strike price*. But the fee you pay for buying the option is *premium*. During the process of considering and stating the *strike price*, what you do is to gamble that the price of a particular asset, which may be a stock, ETFs, etc., will go up or down. And *premium* is the payment you make for the bet, and *a premium* will is always a percentage of the asset's value.

Types of Options

There are two fundamental types of options—call option and put option. These two forms are responsible for offering an investor the right, but not the obligation, to either sell or buy securities. As a beginner who is making an effort to learn options trading, you've got to understand these two forms.

Call Options

Call options are the right an investor has to buy a specific amount of security or financial products at an agreed price over a period of time. In other words, it gives a holder, who is a buyer, to buy the stock. Investors put their money in a call option when they want the security or stock to increase in price. This is how they are able to make a profit off their contract by using their right to purchase the stocks or securities. Remember, I mentioned *premium earlier*. So, the *premium* is the cost you use to buy the contract that will give you the right to eventually buy the security or stock when the time reaches. *The premium* of a call option works like a downpayment you make on security, asset, or stock.

During the purchase of a call option, the seller agrees with you on a specific amount—*strike price*, and you will have the option to buy the asset at an already agreed price, and the price doesn't change until the expiration of the contract. The call option helps you plan for the future. By paying for the contract that will expire later, you are buying an asset at an already decided price, and the price of the asset, security, or stock will not rise even if the price of the asset rises in the market. When you have a lower *strike price* for a call option, you have got a high intrinsic value.

Example of Call Option

We would love to give you a more practical example to show you what the call option really means. Let's use real estate as an example. Mr. A is a potential homeowner, and he sees a development in the desired area, but Mr. A is only willing to exercise the right to own a home in the area when a certain level of development has been achieved. A call option will make this possible for Mr. A. How? If the developer is willing to sell a call option to him. Let's say The developer is willing to sell the home at $500,000 to Mr. A, in the next two years, in the area; the developer will ask Mr. A to buy a call option of, let's say, $50,000. This price is the premium that Mr. A is paying for the *striking price* of $500,000. The $50,000 is non-refundable, and it is a down payment that Mr. A makes to the developer with the expectation that he will buy the asset between now when the contract starts and the next two years when the contract expires.

If two years come, and the area has developed as projected by Mr. A, he can go ahead and pay for the home at $500,000 regardless of the present value of the home, which may be between $700,000 and $900,000. But since he has made a downpayment, the call option gives him the right to it at the agreed price. There is, however, a possible unwanted situation if, for instance, the development approval of the area failed to work out within the space of three years, which is now a year after the expiration of the contract, Mr. A will have to buy the home at the current market price because the call option has expired and in both cases, the developer keeps the *premium:$50,000.*

Put Options

A put option occurs the other way round. It gives an investor the right to sell securities. So, with the put option, you have the right to sell a specific amount of shares, securities, or assets over a certain period. The seller only has the right but not the obligation to sell, and the selling must be done within the contract's expiration date. Strike price and premium also work for put options. The basic difference is that when you buy the put option, you are most likely expecting a fall in the price of the asset. Most importantly, the higher the stake price for a put option, the higher the intrinsic value that the put option has.

Example of a Put Option

For a put option, let's use the stock as an example. A put option works like insurance to protect against risk or loss. So, let's say Mr. A wants to protect his stocks, having seen traces of a possible bear market insight and doesn't want to lose more than 5% of his investments. If the stock is presently trading at $1,250, Mr. A can buy a put option that will give him the right to sell the stocks at $1,000 within the next year. Let's say in the next three months; the market eventually crashes by 40%; Mr. A will make up for his loss by selling his stock at $1,000 when it is trading at $750. If the market doesn't fall within the period, the only loss Mr. A incurs is the premium.

Whether you buy a call or put option, the result is usually with the aim of increasing your money. If you've got the right knowledge to go about it, you would be amazed at how well you would succeed and make tremendous profits.

Why You Should Trade Options

If you don't know the reason you should engage in options trading, we will show you three basic reasons.

Make more money: Who doesn't want to make more money? Well, there is none. We are all working tirelessly every day to achieve our financial goals and live life as we want it. With options trading, you can sell puts or write calls on your shares or assets to make more money while you still have it. In a situation where the stock, for instance, moves above the strike price, by the end of the contract, you may have to buy or sell the stock. Regardless, you have the option premiums as the income you earn.

It helps to hedge risks: With options, you can set certain risk parameters around your securities and assets. Options help you, like insurance, to protect your investments and reduce risks if you are able to use them well. For example, rather than placing a stop-loss order on your stock, you may buy put options to create downside protection for the stock.

It gives room for Speculation: If you capitalize on options, you will be able to leverage and make a bet on moves in whatever direction, whether up, down, or sideways. It gives you access to greater gains (and loses at times.) You don't need a large capital to make high profits with options trading.

Just as it is with every other investment, options trading comes with its risks and benefits. If you are equipped with the basic knowledge and information about how it works, you will find it easy to succeed at putting your resource in options trading. Before we take you deeper into the cores and methods of options trading, let's take a quick tour around some basic terminology you need to familiarize yourself with.

Option Trading Language

Option trading occurs in a wide market, and it involves a wide range of features and strategies. As a result, there are lots of terms that traders use while engaging in options trading. We will not be able to look at all of these terms, but we will definitely look at the basic ones you need to know as a beginner, and as you proceed into the book and trade, you will get to learn more.

Call/call option: It is an option contract that allows you to have the right to buy an asset or security at an agreed price within a certain timeframe.

Put/ put option: It gives you the right to sell assets or securities at a particular point in time over a certain period.

Expiration date: This is the day the option contract becomes inactive. The date depends on the agreement between the seller and buyer.

Break-Even Point: This refers to the price range of underlying assets with no profits or losses.

Bull market: It is used to express that the market, in general, is experiencing growth.

Strike price/ exercise price: It is the price at which you can either buy or sell an asset if you decide to exercise the option.

Premium: It is the price for an option. Premium is made up of intrinsic value and time value.

Intrinsic value: It is the value of the option as a result of the difference between the current market price of a stock and the strike price of the option.

Time value: This is the value of an option as a result of the length of the contract expiration date.

Bear Market: This is used when the market, in general, experiences a decline.

Last: This is the price that was paid or received at the last transaction when the option was traded.

In the money: It is used to express the worth of an option in terms of its intrinsic value. So, this expression shows that the relationship between the asset price in the open market and the strike price favors the contract owner.

Out of the Money: This expression is used to show that there is no financial benefit to exercising the option. So, if the asset price is lower than the strike price, the call option is out of the money. And when the asset price is higher than the strike price, the put option is out of the money.

At the Money: It shows that the asset or stock price is almost equal to the strike price.

Bid: Bid is the amount a buyer has decided to pay for an option. The bid is the premium a seller receives.

Ask: Ask is the amount a seller is willing to receive for an option.

Bullish: It is an expectation that an option, assets, share, or securities will experience an increase in price.

Volume: It is the number of contracts that are traded in a day.

Open interest: This is the amount of options contracts that are in play.

Volatility: It is used to express the measurement of the rate at which an asset price rises and falls every day.

Holder: Rather than the term buyer or seller, options trading has its terms. A holder is an investor who pays for an option to buy an asset or stock within the purview of an agreed contract. A call holder buys an asset, while a put holder sells it.

Writer: The writer refers to the investor who is selling the contract. So, the premium goes to the writer from the holder.

The holder and writer are exposed to risk on a different level. Holders only buy the right to either buy or sell an asset or share. They are not under compulsion to do any. So a holder can decide to exercise the option (which means to buy) or just walk away if they meet with an out-of-the-money situation. The only thing they lose is their premium and the trade commission. However, writers have more to lose. In a situation where the holder is ready to exercise an option, the writer must fulfill the order and sell the asset or shares to the holder regardless of the present market value of the option. As a beginner, it is best to start your options trading as a holder to maximize your profit and learn before you advance. Take your time to have a clear understanding of the basics of options trading. We have got awesome knowledge to divulge.

Chapter Two: Risk and Rewards—Your Playground

Risk is an essential part of every investment, and if you want to go into options trading, you must be ready to face the risks that come with it. Risks shouldn't stop you from investing. You need to be more focused and have a clear-cut plan that you will use to deal with it in order to maximize profits. In general, risks mean the probability of losing money in an investment. Options trading has a high level of risk because there is a possibility of a leveraged loss of trading capital as a result of the leveraged nature of stock options. Ignorance about the risks associated with options trading has been a leading reason many people believe it is a difficult investment to go into. With the right level of information, you will succeed in your training. Let's take you through some pertinent risks that come with options trading.

Primary Risks

Possible Losses

The greatest strength of options trading is the benefit it offers, in that, you can utilize leverage to increase your capital strength. It works in a way that if you purchase a call option of a company's stock that is worth $2,000, there is a probability that you could make so much profit. In case the stock increases, all you've got to do is to invest the $2,000 into the stock. This is the profit it offers, and in this strength lies one of its risks. In a situation where the stock falls or fails to rise but stays still, you will lose your call options and the $2,000. If you had spent $2,000 to buy the stock, you would lose the money only.

The main risk is that the options you buy may expire worthlessly, and this will make you lose all you've invested in the contracts. The same loss is applicable to you if you are writing options. This often happens when the underlying security moves unexpectedly in price. You can deal with this risk by using stop loss orders or by creating spreads.

The Advancement of Options Trading.

Naturally, options trading is a complex form of investment, and this makes it risky. It is not an investment portfolio that anyone will just dabble into. You've got to learn it from the basics to the advanced levels. The truth is, it is quite easy to know the basics, but there are certain aspects and strategies that are hard to use because of their complexities. As a beginner, you may find it hard to understand some of the complex methods. If you are not careful, you are bound to make huge mistakes. But there is also good news about this. Learning about it and the various complex strategies will do the magic.

Time Decay

Time decay is an inevitable risk that comes with option trading. For every option, there is a time value attached to it. The length of the expiration of the contract, the higher the time value. So, when you have options, know that they are losing value as time keeps counting. At times, they may not go down in value, but with time decay, the value of your options may be negatively impacted.

Option is liquid

Now, you can see options being traded by more and more people. This is because investors are getting involved by the day. And with the liquidity state of some options, issues tend to arise. Since there are various forms of options, you are likely to find the options that interest you in low quantity. And this will make it difficult for you to trade because you are most likely going to find it hard to make the required trades at the best prices.

The cost incurred in Trading options

Another risk you are likely to face is in the aspect of the options contract prices. These prices are often quoted on the exchanges, and they go with bid prices and ask prices. The price you get for writing options is the bid price, while the price you pay for buying options is the asking price. Usually, the asking price is higher than the bid price, and there is a difference between the two prices called the bid-ask spread. It is the indirect cost of trading options. The rate of the costs is dependent on how big the spread is. If there is no liquidity, the spreads will be bigger, and this speaks to a high level of risk.

Just like every other form of investment, options trading comes with specific risks. These risks are calculated and can therefore be managed with the right plans and procedures in place. Knowledge is the key you need to trade and minimize the risks you tend to face.

Managing Your Risks

The risks attached to options trading can be managed with the right steps and actions. Let's share some practical ways you can go about this:

Engage in position minimizing: Position minimizing is an effective step to reduce risk and save yourself a lot of money. But how does it work? Whenever you purchase options, you tend to lose the amount you spend to buy the option contract if the option expires without increasing in worth. But with position minimizing, you will deal with this. Position minimizing means you should not spend more than 1% to 2% of your investment capital. So, if your option trading account is made up of $100,000, make sure that the highest option trade you go for is $1,000.

Utilize Fix loss option: Fix loss option comes in handy when you need to cap the total amount of what you lose if any factors work against your short option. It is better to purchase your hedge at the location of the rate you plan to cap your losses at.

Set up a stop loss: Your risk will be in the stock if you sell a covered call. What you need at this point is to set up a stop loss for the position of your stock in places where you need to cut your losses short. And you should buy in order to cover your short call.

You can use a stop loss if you sell a married put. This is because your risk is in the short stock. So, set up a stop loss for the position of your short stock where you will cut your losses short and purchase to close your short put option and cover your short stock.

Avoid putting on option plays that have open risk or those that you cannot define their risks. Exposing yourself to unlimited risk options and those that are uncapped portends a high level of risks. On the negative side, you are likely to lose a lot. So, it is best that you have an exit strategy each time you sell options contracts. You can use option hedges because they work as insurance, and they tend to pay for themselves over a long period of time.

Preparing for risk is your duty as an investor. You cannot do without facing the possibility of losing some amount. But you can protect your money by putting in the hard work. One of the most effective skills you need to manage risk is being able to analyze the options trading market. With these skills, you will be amazed at how well you will excel.

Chapter Three: Becoming a Market Analyst

Understanding how the options trading market works is needed for you to be an effective options trader. The options market is used to explain the total activities of buying and selling of options done globally and in regions. There is a close tie between the option trading market and the stock market. The reason is that stocks are commonly traded forms of options. Also, you have access to options based on some other instrument of finances, which include indices, futures, commodities, and currencies. The options market works on volatility. Your ability to work with this in the market will guide you as you further make decisions on the best strategies to use and those to abandon.

Market Volatility

The options market often runs on the volatility of prices. Volatility refers to the metric of how to price changes in the options market within a period of time. In a situation where market volatility is high, the premium pay for options will be highly expensive, and when the volatility is low, the premiums are very cheap. Volatility is shown in the level of variability that is present in the price changes of financial security, such as a stock or index. The level of the variability shows the rate of volatility. As much as the market can be volatile, there can also be a nonvolatile market. A nonvolatile market is one where there is no change in prices at all, and when changes try to occur, it comes slowly.

In options marketing, volatile trading is possible, and it refers to trading the volatility of a financial instrument instead of trading the original price. When you trade on volatility, you will not be concerned about how the prices move or the direction the prices go. You are only concerned with the movement of the price of the instrument in the future. With options, you can adequately trade on volatility. This is why the predicted future volatility of the underlying instrument of an option is the bedrock of the option's value. If you trade options that are on instruments that come with high levels of future volatility, you have got a valuable option. The expected future volatility value determines the value of the options.

Generally, financial instruments such as stocks, indexes, and more, that are more volatile, often experience changes in their prices. For options, the practical value, which is the extrinsic value, rises or falls based on the expected volatility.

Volatility is an essential element of every financial market. The reason is that lack of volatility will bring about a lack of profit potential in the markets. Volatility is what both investors and traders thrive on. As a beginner, understand that you cannot make any breaks without dealing with volatility. As much as volatility increases the risks that come with options trading, it, at the same time, serves as the basis upon which you can reap good returns from your investment if used well.

There are two types of volatility in the options market.

Historical Volatility

This form of volatility is used to measure the past volatile rate of the market. Historical volatility is often based on a specific period in the past, which may be a year, months, or weeks. The least and standard period of time used for historical calculation volatility is 20 days. The reason is that options trading only occurs twenty days a month. What historical volatility does is annualize the standard deviation of the changes that occurred in price, showing it as a percentage.

Historical volatility is often carried out by determining the average deviation from the average price of a certain financial instrument in a specific period. Standard deviation is the commonest way to calculate historical volatility, and there are other methods you can use. The security risk is dependent on how high the historical volatility value is, and the same rule works for it when it brings good returns. Investors don't use historical volatility for the purpose of measuring the likelihood of losing, but it can be used to do so. It is usually used to measure the distance a security price has from its mean value. If the market is trending, historical volatility helps to measure the distance between the traded prices and the central average, or moving average price. With this, a trending market will experience low volatility even as the prices change over time.

Implied Volatility

This is the second type of volatility. And it refers to the opinion of the market on the volatility of the underlying security of an option. The volatility is determined by certain information, which includes the price of the underlying security (stock, index, futures, etc.), the option's market price, the interest rate, the option's strike price, the option's expiration date, and the dividends. All of these sets of information are determined using different theoretical option pricing models, which include the black Scholes models.

Unlike historical volatility that measures the changes experienced in the past market and the result obtained, implied volatility gives investors the opportunity to predict the future moves, demand, supply and help them employ the predictions in price options contracts. Implied volatility is represented with the *sigma symbol* (σ). At times, it is considered to be a proxy of market risk, and it is expressed commonly through the use of percentages and standard deviations over a certain time horizon. Whenever the implied volatility is applied to the stock market, it goes up in bearish markets, at the point when investors expect equity prices to fall over time. However, it decreases when the market is bullish, and the investors expect the prices to come up over time. For every investor, bearish markets are risky and undesirable. Note that, with implied volatility, you will not gain access to the direction in which the change in price will take. While high volatility shows that there is a large swing in price, it doesn't show whether the price swings up, down, very high, very low, or keeps fluctuating between the two directions. When the volatility is low, it only shows that the price will not likely make unpredictable changes.

Options and Implied Volatility

The pricing of options is dependent on so many factors, of which implied volatility is an essential one. Implied volatility gives an approximate value of the future of an option by taking the current value of the option into consideration. As a result, an investor will pay high premiums for options that have high implied value otherwise for options with low implied volatility. One crucial thing you must note is that implied volatility works on probability. It gives just an estimate of future prices and not an indication of the prices. The truth is, there is no absolute guarantee that the price of the option will follow the predicted pattern. Nonetheless, it offers a handsome help during the consideration for an investment to know the decisions of other investors with options trading, and in a way, since it is correlated with the opinion of the market, it affects options pricing.

Calculating Volatility

As a trader or an investor, you can calculate volatility. To do this, you will have to use variance and standard deviation. The standard deviation is the traditional method of carrying out this measurement. It measures the distance between the current price and the option's mean or moving average. The standard deviation refers to the square root of the variance.

Let's quickly take a glance at this example to have a clear picture of what it means.

Assuming you have a monthly stock with the closing prices of $1 all through $10. What this means is that, for ten months, you have closing prices of your stock with a $1 increase: In the first month, you have $1, second month, you get $2, month 3, you get $3, month 4, you get $4 until you reach $10. You can calculate the variance of this stock by using these steps below:

Start by identifying the mean of the data set: What this means is that you will add each value and divide it by the number of the value.

So, you will add $1 to $2 to $3 to $4 until you get to $10. With this, you will have $. Then, you will divide it by $10 since you have got 10 numbers in your data set. So, you will have a mean or an average price of $5.50.

Do the calculation of the differences that exist between every data value and the mean or average price: This calculation is what is referred to as deviation. So, you will calculate this way:

Take $10 - $5.50 = $4.50

Take $9 - $5.50 = $3.50

Take $8 - $5.50 = $2.50

You will keep doing this until you reach the first data value of $1. Note that you will get negative numbers, and it is fine because you need all of the values. once you are done with these steps for each of the values, do the following:

Square each of the deviations, and you will easily do away with the negative values.

Now, add all the squared deviations, and in the example above, you will get 82.5.

Then, divide the total of all the squared deviations, which is 82.5, by the number of data values (10 in this example.) You will get $8.25 as the variance, and then you will take the square root of this value to get the standard deviation. The Standard deviation then is $2.87.

With this calculation, you have measured the risk and expressed how values can be spread out around the mean or average price. Traders and investors will know the possible distance the price can go from the average price. You can check the table below for the input of the example above.

	A	B	C	D	E	F
1	Price	Mean	Deviation	Deviation Squared	Variance	Standard Deviation
2	1	5.5	-4.5	20.25		
3	2	5.5	-3.5	12.25		
4	3	5.5	-2.5	6.25		
5	4	5.5	-1.5	2.25		
6	5	5.5	-0.5	0.25		
7	6	5.5	0.5	0.25		
8	7	5.5	1.5	2.25		
9	8	5.5	2.5	6.25		
10	9	5.5	3.5	12.25		
11	10	5.5	4.5	20.25		
12	55			82.5	8.25	2.872281323

(investopedia.com)

Trading Volatility

As mentioned earlier, investors and traders who trade volatility are not concerned about the price movement direction. Their target is to make a profit on increased volatility regardless of whether it rises or falls. You can use the Straddle strategy to take advantage of volatility in the market with the use of options.

Straddle Strategy with Options

The straddle strategy works well with options to trade volatility. Using options to trade volatility involves the trader buying a call option and a put option using the same strike price and expiration date. In this case, if there is a large price shift in the underlying instruments, both the call option and put option will be in-the-money for the trader and investor. Also, if the price rises, the call option brings in profits, and if the price falls, the put option brings money for the investor.

Take a look at the graph below:

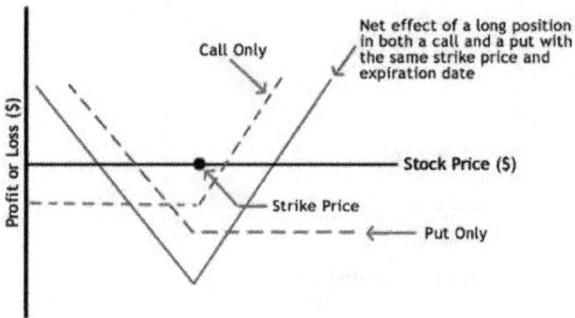

(mytradingskills.com)

In the graph above, an investor or trader can only lose if both the call and put options fail to yield. But if the price keeps moving away from the strike price in any of the directions, the investor enjoys profit. As we have mentioned from the beginning of this book that, as much as there are risks associated with options trading, there are lots of profits attached to investing in it as long as you do it with the right knowledge. You can also trade volatility using the straddle strategy and pending orders. There is no doubt that your ability to trade volatility is needed for you to enjoy great profit from the options trading market. Knowing the way to do it and how to do it is the right information you need.

Chapter Four: Creating a Trading Plan

Planning is an essential factor we must all consider to be successful in life. If you fail to plan, you will act without direction, and this easily impedes success more than any other act. Every successful investor understands the need to plan out their investments to make profits. Planning your trading will give you the strength to be consistent and achieve your target. Many people don't take options trading seriously, and hence, they couldn't enjoy the benefits that come with trading options. Success in trading options doesn't come overnight. It requires proper planning and thorough homework.

Your options trading plan will outline the method you will adopt to trade, the amount you want to spend on the options, the level of risk you want to take, and you will have a measurement to know your overall performance. As a beginner, starting with a solid plan in mind will make you achieve success faster than you might have thought. As a trader, you've got to put all of yourself to execute your trade edge and, importantly, ensure you commit the plan to paper.

Why You Need a Plan

Emotion is a leading cause of failure in trading. Emotions can set in when you either make a profit or loss big. It gives your mind a certain spinning nature that may make you change your strategy and plans. But with a trading plan, you will be in check. Trading plans will present methodical instructions to you on how you can handle every situation that may arise during your trading. Also, you will have a guide on how you should handle multiple trades. Situations may get you anxious and lead to you losing out on certain opportunities, but with the help of your plans, you will know what to do at every point in time. Another benefit of setting up a trading plan is that it offers you the opportunity to know what will work and what won't work. If you are into random trading where you just buy and sell whatever options you see, it won't work for you effectively. But when you target the right options, and you monitor your progress, you will have an awesome result.

Preplanning Your Trading

Achieving success in options trading is not about creating a trading plan but about creating an effective plan. To do this, you've got to take some steps ahead of planning. You have to make some considerations and let them guide your choice. Let's take you through some things you've got to consider before you start planning.

Identify the best trading that works for your personality. There are various forms of trading, and all of these types work for different personalities. For example, if you are an active person, you can consider trading styles that involve daily activities, such as day trading or short-term trading.

Select the market you want to trade. You can choose among forex, stocks binary options, or any other security. If possible, you may combine. Just note that each of these markets has its pros and cons. But your plan will be based on your choice of market.

Identify your trading objectives. Know the reason you are trading. It is not enough to trade options just because you want to make more money. It may be that you want to make $100,000 in a year or buy a car. It may be that you want to make money to pay your kids' college tuition or anything. So, your trading plan should provide a means through which you want to achieve your objectives. Your objectives will always motivate you to persevere and keep trying, and at the same time, they will guide you on how best you can make trading decisions based on the available resources.

Creating Your Trading Plan

Every trading plan is personalized. The reason is that every trader thinks differently. Your trading plan will reflect your trading style, the level of your risk tolerance, and your preferences. This is why it is always advised that you take your time to set your trading plan yourself. You don't need the help of anyone. Just follow the basic components in this section and craft an awesome and result-driven plan for yourself.

Create Your Goals

Goals are needed to be the basis of your trading plan. Before you put your money into any trade or purchase that put or call options, ensure you have your goals analyzed and written out. Your goals should show your profit target. Make sure this is realistic. It will show the minimum risk you can take. What is the potential profit range for you to trade? There are traders who only trade when they see that the potential profit is twice or thrice greater than the risk in probability. Your goals can be weekly, monthly, or yearly. You've got to create time to re-assess them.

State your Risk Level

You've got to be intentional about this aspect of trading. Know the amount of your portfolio you can risk on a single trade. So, your risk tolerance level will determine this. The risk rate often varies depending on the trade, but ideally, it should only range between 1% and 5% of your portfolio every trading day. So, if you lose the amount you set in a day, you take a pause on trading for the day. A good way to trade is to know when to back down and re-strategize before you lose too much.

Do a Background Check

Traders are ardent learners and researchers. Before the market opens, ensure you read about the activities going on around the world. Know how the global market is faring. Know whether S&P 500 index futures are up or down in pre-market. This knowledge will help you gauge the mood of the market before the market opens because future contracts trade every time—day and night.

Be Prepared for Trade

Regardless of the trading system you are using, ensure you label minor and major support and resistance levels on the charts. Have your alert set for the entry and exit signals and set it in a way that you are sure you can see all signals or detect it with an audible auditory signal and clear visual signal.

Guide your entry point

Don't trade without setting entry rules. The entry rules should be simple that they will aid the possibility of making snap decisions. Set less subjective conditions when you set out to trade so that you won't find the whole process difficult. An entry rule could be:

If Signal X increases and there is the least target of nothing less than three times as high as my stop loss, I will buy Y contracts or shares here. You've got to be like a computer when it comes to abiding by your entry rules. Ensure that if the conditions you set are met, you make the move that follows. Don't be emotional about it.

Know when to exit by rules

Don't fall into the pit of seeking only the right signal of when to trade. Ensure you also pay attention to knowing the right time to exit. It is common among traders to find it hard to sell when they are down, all because they are afraid of losing. As a trader, who wants to be successful, learn to be strong and accept losses as they come because they are part of what makes trading work. What you need to do is identify your exit strategy right before you enter into a trade. Every trade gives at least two exits. The first is for you to know your stop loss if the trade doesn't go as you planned. Write down your stop loss, and don't just rely on your mental strength. Another exit strategy you should surely have is a profit target. Once you reach your profit target, sell a part of your position and move the stop loss over the other position up to the point of breakeven.

Record and Performance Analysis

Your plan should contain the system you want to adopt to record your trading activities. Your records should include listing the moments you had great wins, what you did right and how you did it. The same rules apply when you lose. Note why you lose and how. It will prevent you from making further mistakes along the line. Also, have a record of your target, and observe your entry rule and exit strategy. Your trading records should always be kept and saved for future analysis.

You have got to know that your effectiveness is not measured when you only keep records. The records are kept for a purpose—to check for future analysis of your performance. Know your loss or gains in the business, identify your mistakes and retrace them.

Being a success at options trading is a journey that you must be consistent on. You need to be resolute and make adequate preparation. Planning your trading activities will not only help you achieve success, but it will also make the whole process of trading easy and smooth. You will be able to monitor your progress and know where you need assistance. Planning ahead before trading will place you in a fast lane as an options trader.

Chapter Five: Adopting the Right Strategy

When people say that options trading is difficult and complex, they are not really lying. It is just that they fail to tell the truth about the need to understand the available strategies that can be adopted. There are several options trading strategies that you've got to know as a beginner who really wants to be successful in investing. Each of these strategies will give you the capacity to limit your risk and maximize your returns. Your knowledge of the right strategies to adopt will guide you and help you make informed decisions. It makes the whole process of investing easy and perfect. Let's take you through the strategies you need to know.

Covered Call

A covered call is a popular strategy used by many investors. It involves buying a naked option. Investors have the opportunity to buy-write or structure a covered call. This strategy is adopted by many investors because it helps to make more profits and has a low risk of staying longer on the stock alone. But note the trade-off behind this strategy. You have got to be willing to sell your security at a specific price, which is the short strike price.

Here is how the strategy works. Suppose you use a call option on a stock that is equivalent to 1000 shares of stock for every call option. If you buy 1000 shares, at the same time, you will sell one call option against it. It is called a covered call because it helps you if the price of the stock rises dramatically. Your short call will be covered by the long stock position. This strategy helps investors when they have a short-term position in a stock, and they don't have a definite opinion on how it is moving, So, they want to generate income by selling the call premium or by placing a protective measure around it in order to forestall a possible decline in the stock's value.

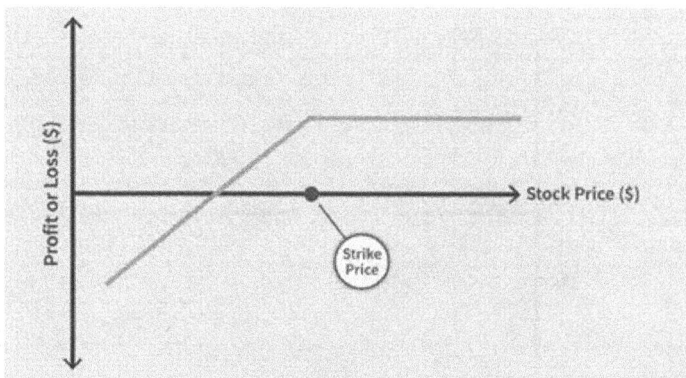

Covered Call Strategy

The covered call strategy graph above explains it clearly. As the price of the stock rises, the negative profit and loss that arise from the call are offset by the long share position. When the investor sells the call, the premium received gives the investor the opportunity to sell the stock at a higher rate than the strike price as the stock moves through the strike price to the upside. The result for the investor is the strike price and the premium received.

Married Put

For this strategy, you buy an asset, which may be a share, and at the same time place put options for the same number of shares. The holder of a put option can always sell the stock at the strike price. This strategy helps investors to protect their downside risk while they hold a stock. It helps to create a floor in case the price of the stock falls drastically. While this strategy helps an investor on the possible downside, it has a potential negative impact. If the value of the stock fails to fall, the investor will lose the premium paid for the put option.

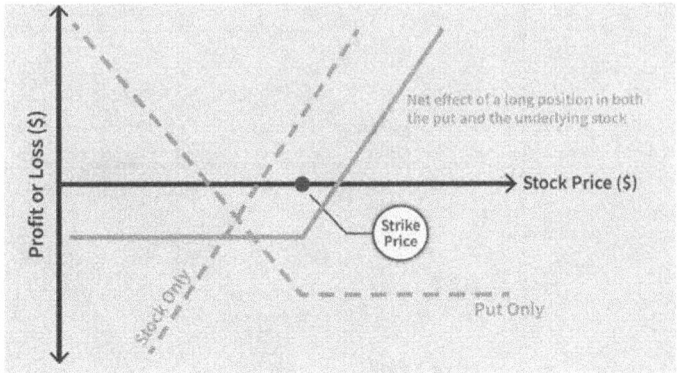

The Married Put Strategy

The graph shows the long stock position, which is represented by the dashed line. The long put and long stock positions are combined, and as the price of the stock falls, the losses are not high. But the stock is seen working in the upside more than the premium spent for the put.

Bull Call Spread

This strategy involves an investor buying calls at a given strike price and at the same time selling the calls at a much higher strike price. Investors use this strategy when they are sure that the price of the call will increase. The simultaneously sold call options will possess the same underlying asset and expiration date. With this strategy, you can easily reduce your upside on the trade and reduce the net premium you will spend. The Bull call strategy is a bullish strategy.

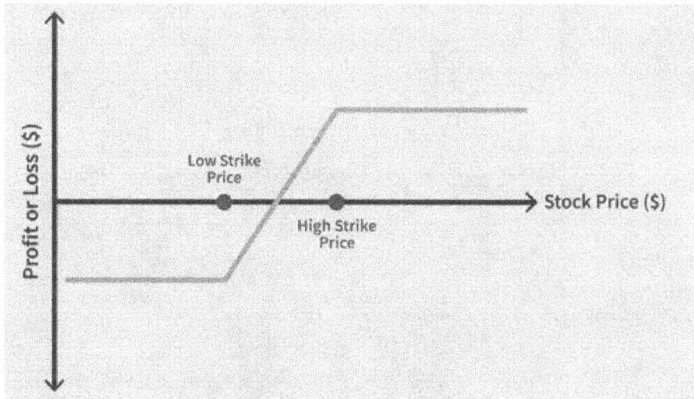

The Bull Call Spread Strategy

This graph explains how the strategy works. For you to be successful at using the strategy, you have to give room for the price of the stock to increase so you can make a profit when you trade. This strategy comes with a trade-off, and that is the fact that your upside is limited, despite the fact that the amount you spend on the premium is low. This strategy is set up in a way that when outright calls become high in price, you've got a way to offset the higher premium, which is for you to sell higher strike calls against them.

Bear Put Spread Strategy

This strategy is a form of vertical spread. It allows you to buy put options at a certain strike price, and you sell the put at a lower strike price simultaneously. Investors use this strategy when they have a bearish sentiment about the asset and have the opinion that the price of the asset will fall. With this strategy, the investor will experience both limited losses and limited gains.

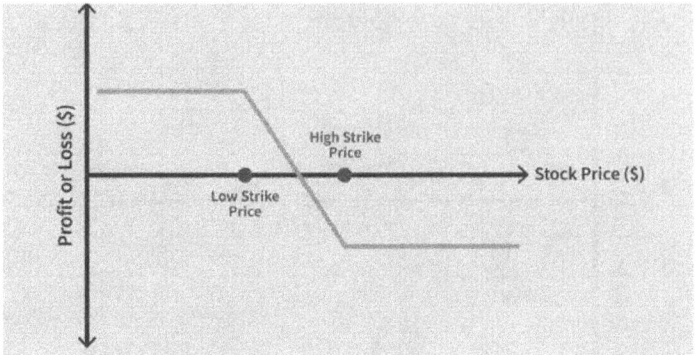

Bear Put Spread Strategy

The graph above explains the strategy. For you to be successful using this strategy, the underlying asset price must fall. This strategy makes your upside limited while your premium is also reduced. In a situation where the outright puts are expensive, you can sell lower strike puts against them to offset the high premium.

Protective Collar

This strategy involves buying an out-of-the-money put option and at the same time writing an out-of-the-money call option. For this trading, the underlying asset and the expiration are expected to be the same. Investors use this strategy when a long position in stock brings about substantial gains. So, with this strategy, the investor enjoys downside protection while the long put locks the possible sale price. However, the investor may have to sell shares at a higher price, which will likely lead to letting go of possible profits to be made in the future.

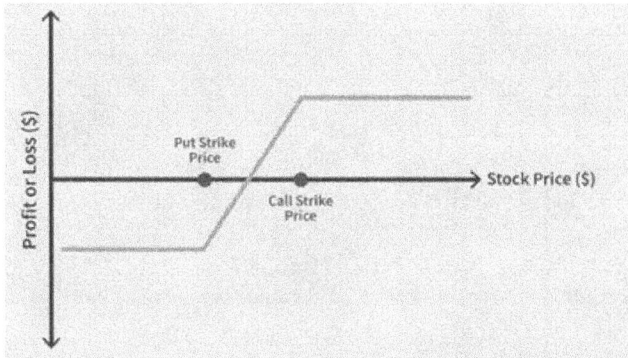

Protective Collar Strategy

In the above graph, you will see the protective collar. It is a combination of a covered call and a long put. This strategy protects the investor if there is a fall in the price of the stock, and while the investor may be forced to sell the long stock at the short call strike, there is a place of happiness in the sense that the investor already enjoyed gains in the shares.

Long Strangle

The long strangle strategy involves an investor buying an out-of-the-money call and put option that shares the same underlying asset and similar expiration date at the same time. A trader uses this strategy with the expectation that the underlying asset's price will grow; however, the trader doesn't know the exact direction it will take. The graph below explains it better. You will see two breakeven points. This strategy brings profits when the stock rises in either direction.

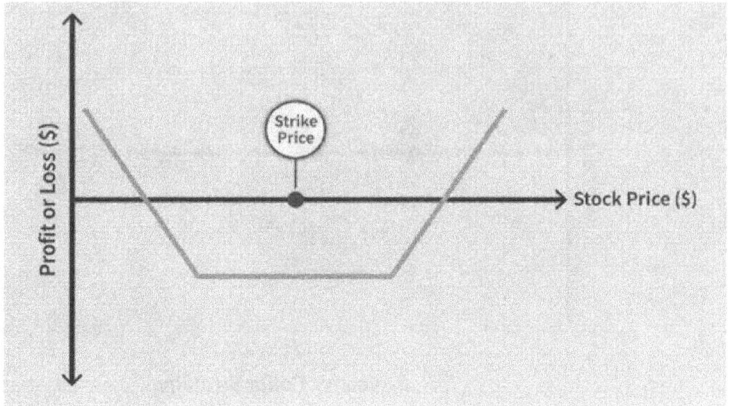

The Long Strangle Strategy

Long Call Butterfly Spread

This strategy involves the combination of a bull spread strategy and a bear spread strategy. It also involves the use of three different strike prices. The options are all for a single underlying asset and expiration date. A trader can buy a one-in-the-money call option at a low price and sell two in-the-money call options, and at the same time buy one out-of-the-money call option.

For the long call butterfly spread, the maximum gain is made when the stock doesn't change until expiration, which is the point of an at-the-money (ATM) strike. The longer the distance of the stock from the ATM strikes, the greater the negative change in the profit and loss of the trade. Note that the highest loss can occur only when the stock settles at the lower strike or below it. With this strategy, you will enjoy limited upside and downside.

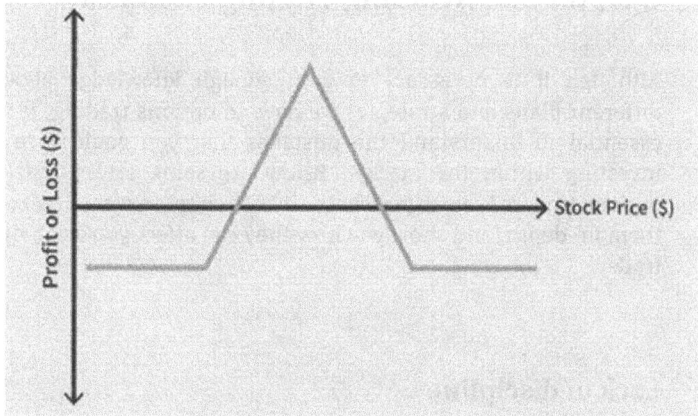

Long Call Butterfly Spread

Becoming a successful options trader involves consistent learning. The more you trade, the better you become at it, and the more you know, the better result you get. The strategies you can use to trade options are numerous, and you can keep learning more as you are immersed in trading. The key to becoming a better trader is to learn, do your research, and keep trading. As a beginner, your greatest fear should be to look for ways you can avoid mistakes as you trade. So, we have prepared basic information you need to prevent yourself from falling in your attempts. The next chapter will put you through how to avoid mistakes as you trade.

Chapter Six: Avoiding Trading Mistakes

Although it is necessary to gain enough knowledge about the different plans and strategies we have in options trading, it is also essential to understand the mistakes that you could face while investing within the market. Below are some errors that many options traders have experienced. In this chapter, we will talk about them in-depth, and show you how they can affect you as an options trader.

Lack of discipline

Many criteria fall under this. Different types of traders can lack discipline regardless of their knowledge level. You could be an experienced trader or an inexperienced trader that was taught by a very successful trader—who has taught you all you need to be a good trader and make money. Lack of discipline refers to traders who do not follow the rules and guidelines and prefer to take shortcuts to achieve bottom-line success; as I mentioned earlier, high win-rates do not signify an excellent trader. Ill-disciplined traders would be after getting a high win rate and would no doubt lack the courage to maximize profit yielding trades. Lack of discipline creates a fake aura of overconfidence and a phony sense of entitlement which would make them ignore their losses or look for ways to reduce them. The entitlement mentality would make them think they are overdue for a winning trade and make them forget money management principles. Such traders would pump money into a trade immediately after suffering losses in the hope of recovering their losses quickly, forgetting that the results of previous trades will not in any way affect the results of the next trade.

Wrong thinking about profit

The factors that help determine bottom-line profitability when buying options are win rate, average win, and average loss. All option buyers should aim for a win rate below 50% because you will be expected to pay a time premium that will reduce at a non-linear rate. You are also expected to make your market moves within a time frame; otherwise, you risk losing it because of its expiration date. The above factors make options trading less dependent on a high win rate as the main guarantee for profits is an average win rate that is higher than the average loss. This implies that you should maximize any opportunity for gains and always look for ways to reduce your losses if it is possible. High rates are misleading in options trading because it implies such traders are not effective in all opportunities and such kinds are prone to hold on losing trades, hoping it makes them become winners, which is a recipe for disaster.

Lack of diversification in your portfolio

Diversification in options trading applies to many aspects, from the strategies to plans, etc. Make it a priority to be aware of all the unknowns and how to react in different market environments. There are some strategies that apply to specific market conditions better than others, such as Straddles: A strategy that enables you to make significant gains from explosive moves in both directions without hindering the growth of your spreads. Also, there are other premium-selling strategies that bring in profits for you in an environment without directions. If you decide to use option trading as your only option, you can still make it as diverse as possible to maximize the gains that you can receive. Diversifying under an option buying strategy means you are exposed to both calls and puts them at different time frames. It gives you a setup for both call and put trades that can be used until your time is expired. A call set up could contain a break-out strategy that works based on momentum and a good strategy that searches for an oversold situation where the underlying is already going back to support.

Trading without an edge

Trading is a competitive journey that follows the standard rules of competitions. For example, the reason why tracks in relay races are staggered is to create a level playing field for all athletes. Imagine if the runner on the last lap that has the shortest distance in the center starts his or her race level with the first, it creates an advantage over others. This is what you should look for in options trading. What information do you have that others do not? What can you think of that most cannot? How can you turn privileged information into money-making opportunities or trades? You would only be able to maximize your chances if you have an edge that you can turn into a signal that can direct you on the possible movements of the market. Advantages in options trading involve getting hints about the direction of an underlying opportunity that the majority are oblivious to; or an open interest configuration; or the prices of many options that make the risk-reward attractive.

Misallocation of capital

There are many opportunities that would arise when you want to buy options. There are some that could present a chance to multiply your capital in many folds within a short time and make very significant gains. However, these opportunities could also cause you to lose all your capital if you choose the wrong option. So, when investing in high-risk trades that have the same possibilities for an increase or loss, make sure you do not commit all your funds to it. Leave more funds to trade with stocks than you commit to such trading options as it gives you a chance to maximize both opportunities. As a stock trader, you have the possibility to earn similar profits without undertaking excessive risks. Always give yourself the option to recover from losses and to not stake your entire portfolio on a short-term opportunity.

Poor option selection

There are many available directions that can be used by options traders. These include the numerous strike prices that are available with their time of expiration. Each available route has its own advantages and disadvantages. The benefit consists of the flexibility and capability to make your indicator work within the time frame where your move is expected to occur. A disadvantage is that availability of multiple options could be overwhelming for new and inexperienced traders. All traders can manage risks differently, and the type of options you will buy must go hand in hand with your risk tolerance ability. There are trades that offer more profits but come with the possibility of losing your entire investment. Such trades should be used with strike selection that will determine when the exercise price would become effective, especially when the trade is nearing expiration. The strike price and the time of expiration must be considered when selecting an option. The time frame must be aligned with indicators when trading options.

Mistakes are part of our life experiences. We grow with them if we are calculative enough. As a trader, your trading mistakes can either make or mar you. If you make the right mistakes, you will find yourself rising up and getting back on your feet. But the wrong mistake will stop you from ever trying to invest or trade again.

Conclusion

Options trading is a good way to build your wealth if done correctly. It offers you passive income that will help you achieve your financial goals. While many people believe that options trading is complex and difficult to achieve, successful, experienced investors and traders are making their money. We have provided you with the basic knowledge you need to build wealth around options trading. The information we have given will guide you as you make your debut, and as much as you learn and trade, you will become familiar with advanced and complex strategies you can use to become a pro as a trader. There is no better way to increase your money than to make it work for you. Learn the process now, and start making money as an options trader.

If you enjoyed this book in anyway, an honest review is always appreciated!